SHROPSHIRE'S
Historic
PUBS

SHROPSHIRE'S
HISTORIC
PUBS

JAN DOBRZYNSKI

The
History
Press

Martha Rhoden's Tuppenny Dish – Morris dancers performing at the White Horse, Clun, during the annual Green Man Festival heralding the coming of spring with three days of music, dance and entertainment.

Lines from *A Shopshire Lad* are reproduced by kind permission of the Society of Authors as the literary representative of the Estate of A.E. Housman.

First published 2009

Reprinted 2011, 2012, 2013

The History Press
The Mill, Brimscombe Port
Stroud, Gloucestershire, GL5 2QG
www.thehistorypress.co.uk

British Library Cataloguing in Publication Data.
A catalogue record for this book is available from the British Library.

ISBN 978 0 7509 5118 0

Typesetting and origination by The History Press
Printed in Great Britain

CONTENTS

The Boat Inn, a perfect example of a picturesque Shropshire pub in a pleasant garden setting.

The perfect example of a historic pub: the Kings Head at Bridgnorth.

PREFACE

With over 650 to choose from and hundreds visited, the task of selecting a representative number of historic pubs in Shropshire was far from easy, especially since this perfect embodiment of an English county has so many unique establishments worthy of mention. The search to find the choicest pubs took me through all of the county's towns and villages, along its rivers and over the rugged Shropshire Hills and along Shropshire's lost and forgotten highways and byways.

There were certainly more pubs found than could be put into this book, but sixty of the total number were selected as a fair choice. All are representative of the many different styles of hostelry and are dispersed throughout the whole county. Included here are establishments of the highest standard that capture the essence of the wayside inn, the local, riverside mug house, railway and canal pub as well as the increasingly popular brewery tap house. Suffice it to say that the pubs featured in this book are among the best in Shropshire and all certainly have a history and perhaps a tale of the unusual, or even the supernatural. Having visited them on many occasions, they are all heartily recommended to anyone in search of good beer, good food, a warm welcome and a historical setting.

Jan Dobrzynski, 2009

The ancient fire symbol and one of the oldest inn signs, symbolising warmth, light, and vitality.

The Powis Arms, Lydbury North, with a delightfully welcoming doorway, tempting customers to enter.

INTRODUCTION

Oh I have been to Ludlow fair,
And left my necktie God knows where,
And carried half way home, or near,
Pints and quarts of Ludlow beer . . .

A.E. Housman, *A Shropshire Lad*, 1896

Every pub has its own history and architectural features that make it unusual or unique. Old or modern, the pub has a function and a purpose beyond that of just a place to drink and eat. Every pub offers a place for people to meet, talk, show friendship, or conduct business, but above all, a place to feel comfortable and relaxed in. Shropshire's historic pubs belong to a county that is unique and distinct, largely agricultural, a cattle-, sheep- and cereal-growing region, but also famous throughout the world as the birthplace of the industrial age.

As a county, Shropshire has a rich and varied history spanning centuries and its pubs reflect a small part of the social and cultural changes brought about by major historic events. The alehouse was ever-present as Romans, Saxons, Danes and then Normans left their mark on the area. By the time Shrewsbury had grown to be the county's only substantial town, allied to a string of castles along the Marches (a contested border region fought over by the Welsh and English for centuries), the alehouse was commonplace. With the Act of Union in 1536, the conflict between England and Wales was finally resolved and Shropshire settled down to a relatively peaceful and prosperous time, only disrupted by the start of the Civil War in 1642. For all this time ale had been a staple drink and a necessity for good health and wellbeing. By the Middle Ages brewing and drinking was an established practise throughout Shropshire and the British Isles as a whole.

The ancient symbol of the alehouse: a bundle of branches, held by Vanessa – a modern day alewife to Sir John Savile's Household, member of the Wars of the Roses Federation.

The misericords in Ludlow's Parish Church of St Laurence depict scenes of contemporary life in 1447. The figure nicknamed 'Simon the cellarer' (perhaps fuddled with drink) is drawing ale from a barrel.

Ale was often purchased and drunk at a 'church ale', an event held by the church which was typically a festival for a religious occasion or for the collection of tithes. However, increasingly in the Middle Ages ale was sold and drunk in the tavern and inn. The more sophisticated inns and taverns offered ale, wine, spirits, food and accommodation for travellers while the monasteries and religious houses disappeared or declined under the Protestant Reformation, and ceased to brew and sell ale for the weary traveller and pilgrim. Eventually the 'church ales', along with festivals and religious plays, disappeared and the church was no longer the communal focus for the town and village – or the place for merriment and drinking

During the reign of the Tudors and Stuarts, the alehouse, inn and tavern increasingly became the social centre of every community, hamlet, village and town. These establishments offered entertainment: music and singers, actors and exotic performing animals, with freak shows appearing on occasion. The customers themselves played games such as cards, dice, backgammon and draughts or took part in outdoor activities and sports such as football and bowls. The alehouse became a social centre, a place to meet and make friends, shelter from the weather and escape from the daily toil, or in some establishments, male customers might call on the services of a prostitute. The alehouse also catered for social occasions and feasts, christenings, funerals and the marriage feast. It was also during this period of history that beer (brewed with hops for flavour and as a preservative) became popular.

Shropshire changed dramatically during the Industrial Revolution, with new industries and houses built to accommodate their workers. The expansion of the canals, roads and railways changed the shape of the landscape. In this time of rapid change, beer was still the only safe drink, not contaminated and deadly, so jugs or pots of beer were brought to quench the thirst and revive workers in the fields and factories. Increasingly, drinking establishments which sold beer became more specialised. Many were purpose-built to supply a particular type of customer: mug houses that catered for the river trade, the posting and stagecoach inns with beds available twenty-four hours a day, drovers' hostelry, canal side inn, railway inn and local.

In eighteenth-century England, 'Drunk for a penny' was the drinkers' phrase, since no licence was required to serve spirits and duty was only *2d* a gallon. Raw spirits, like gin, were consumed in increasingly large quantities. By the middle of the century, one-fifth of drinking houses were gin shops. Taxes, legislation governing the sale of spirits and increases in grain prices ended the era of gin alley and the drunkenness of the masses. The alehouse also changed and with the 1830 Public Premises Act, which permitted a private house to sell beer (but not spirits) on payment of two guineas to the Customs & Excise, thousands of 'public houses' took the opportunity to open their doors to the public. The name 'pub' was first used to describe these new establishments and most brewed their own beer.

The pub inevitably became more popular and profitable, and proprietors found it was more expedient to buy their beer than to brew it themselves, leading to the formation of local breweries in the towns and villages of Shropshire. Most of these brewing concerns began to compete with each other, merge and take over other smaller concerns, inevitably resulting in the formation of large regional breweries. These breweries began to buy pubs and install their own tenants and managers to ensure their beer was the only source of supply. Continued mergers ultimately brought about the eventual disappearance of most of the breweries in Shropshire, leaving most pubs tied to familiar national names like Allsops, Bass, Banks's, Charrington, Courage, Tetley, Whitbread and Worthington. In 1989, government orders required breweries to limit the size of their tied estate, which resulted in the sale of many pubs to pubcos (property holding investment companies owning a large chain of several thousand pubs).

The Three Tuns' Victorian brewery tower, Bishop's Castle.

An ornate fireplace, railway relics and pictures on the walls contribute to the ambiance of the Railwaymans Arms – a traditional railway pub.

As a result, many pubs in Shropshire – tied and free houses – have suffered some unsympathetic alterations to either the whole building or the interior. Tied houses have probably suffered the greatest ruination in the name of improvement by the hand of brewery and pubco. While it is accepted some changes are necessary (e.g. to comply with access, fire and safety legislation), other changes are a result of misguided attempts to improve profits and turnover or introduce a corporate image in the belief that every pub owned by the chain should look like every other pub owned by the chain. Recent trends are to create factory-style drinking and eating emporia equipped with children's wacky play areas and, far worse, conversion to a theme pub or a pretentious gastro pub. The pubs that have remained independent free houses, privately owned and free from the interference of the breweries or pubcos, have fared better. The free house pub has not fallen victim to the corporate makeover like the tied properties but many have suffered in other ways. The most common despoilment is the opening up of individual rooms and spaces, the inclusion of a single central bar, intrusive dining areas and the removal of fireplaces. Other eyesores are fake beams and heavily textured ceilings and walls. Carpets laid over oak floors or stone tiles and blocked-off serving hatches also detract from a pub's appearance. The pub interior makeover is an alteration which seldom works and inevitably detracts from the appearance of a historic pub. It usually hides or ruins a fine architectural feature or nuance, removing intimacy and character. The makeover is a fad, which lacks permanence and soon starts to look dated, tired, then run-down and neglected while an unaltered interior remains authentic.

Despite this, Shropshire still has many excellent historic pubs. Most of the pubs I visited during the course of my research were of a high standard with publicans, landlords, managers and staff polite and eager to make you feel welcome. So how then have the pubs included here been selected? In the first instance, they must be pubs and not hotels (whose main purpose is to provide accommodation) or eateries (where catering takes precedence over drinking), nor coffee houses, town bars, restaurants or bistros although these distinctions are often blurred. I have omitted pubs where the fabric of the building has changed out of all recognition or when documented history is all that remains. Similarly, being the oldest pub in the town or the village does not guarantee selection, especially if the pub lacks real historical features, a sense of community or does not sell real ale. Indeed, stringent criteria are used to gauge whether or not a pub justifies inclusion. Firstly, they must be pubs within the county boundary, i.e. the ceremonial county of Shropshire, made up of the six municipal boroughs and unitary authorities of Bridgnorth, South Shropshire, Telford & Wrekin, Shrewsbury & Atcham, North Shropshire and Oswestry. Secondly, each pub must serve real ale, which is cask-conditioned and not pasteurised and forced out of the keg by gas from a cylinder. A large proportion of the original interior and exterior must survive intact, and the pub must have genuine features and ideally some folklore. Finally, the atmosphere must be congenial and welcoming with the staff cheerful and pleasant, relaxed and unhurried. Very often pubs have truculent, impatient staff, too busy, overworked or reluctant to talk to a customer and constantly willing the customer to take his beer, eat his meal and go – a feature of many pubco canteens and rowdy youth-orientated bars where a customer is merely units per hour sales.

A good pub must have cheery, welcoming staff as here at the Cock Hotel, Wellington, Telford.

When I started my research for this book, it was estimated by CAMRA (February 2007) that on average fifty-six pubs close every month in the UK. At the conclusion of my research (February 2009) various estimates put the figure at 150 closures a month. There will always be pubs in Shropshire, but the question to ask is what they will be like. Few pubs are commercially safe and free from the threat of closure. Many pubs are on a stay of execution, in limbo, closed and boarded-up and awaiting a decision on change of use by the council, or awaiting inevitable dereliction to a point when demolition is the only option. Many pubs will close, of which 80 per cent will be demolished and the site on which they stand given over to developers. Pubs of historic interest – listed by English Heritage – might avoid that fate and be subject to an enquiry and planning review. Local protest and campaign against permanent closure might reprieve a few, and provided someone is prepared to buy or lease them, they will reopen again as a licensed public house. Others will have change of use granted and will be sold and used for something else.

The reasons for closures are complex and many theories and opinions are voiced as to why pubs close. Some explanations are obvious but others are the result of long-standing social trends which, in some instances, go back to the nineteenth century. Regarding recent closures, comments from Shropshire landlords, brewers, pubco representatives and the drinking public during my research visits, suggest that excessively high beer prices, cheap supermarket beer, high taxes, the smoking ban, bad summers and recession are primary causes.

The Sun Inn, Clun, one of Shropshire's pubs at risk, closed in January 2009 and awaiting a rescue plan.

The last pub in the village: the Kynnersley Arms, Leighton, closed in 2008, its fate unknown as it falls derelict.

The last pub in the village: the Wheatsheaf, Soudley (Market Drayton), closed for many years, awaiting demolition and redevelopment for rural housing.

Many people apportion blame to the pubco financial model: pubcos borrowing heavily, securing against their pubs and dropping properties to reduce long-term debt to ensure future bond repayments. Many pubs are losing customers while their owners scramble for credit and cash by increasing rents to tenants and leaseholders in an attempt to offset diminishing returns. It is not surprising that the pub as an institution is under threat. The free house on the other hand, although hit hard by loss of trade, has fared better than brewery-owned and pubco premises and is likely to survive for some time.

A reader wishing to visit the pubs mentioned here may like to note that pubs no longer have fixed opening hours. Consequently many do not open until late afternoon or early evening. Some remain closed for one or two days a week, some unfortunately may have closed for good. Anyone intending to visit an unfamiliar pub should telephone or access the pub's website for opening times. The telephone number and website addresses are at the head of each entry along with postcodes for the benefit of motorists with satellite navigation. Also included are directions on foot, mention of public transport when available and parking. Pub entries in each chapter are listed alphabetically by village or town followed by the pub entry, also in alphabetical order.

The success story, pubs survive in Shropshire's isolated rural communities by offering additional services to the local community. The fighting Cocks at Stottesdon has won many awards for its high standards, and praise from all who care about the rural way of life.

Right: The Fighting Cocks function-room is an asset to the village offering meeting facilities for local organisations, veterinary advice, parties and gatherings.

A romantic view of the Boathouse Inn, a perfect setting for one of Shropshire's historic pubs on the banks of the River Severn at Shrewsbury. (*Publisher unidentified*) (Author's collection)

The Boat House Inn in the 1930s. (*Excel Series*) (Author's Collection)

The enticing entrance to the Brewery Tap at the Kings Head, Bridgnorth.

ONE

Brew Pubs

The Romans probably introduced brewing of ale to the area in the villas and Tabernae at Viroconium (Wroxeter) or Mediolanum (Whitchurch). When they left, the Saxon, Danish and Norman invaders carried on the brewing and drinking tradition. After 1066, the Normans settled down in Saxon England and started to build their castles, monasteries and churches in the newly formed county of Shropshire. Many of these institutions, secular and ecclesiastical, had the obligatory brewhouse attached, since ale, which by then had become a staple drink for young and old alike, was infinitely more preferable to the often-contaminated water from streams and wells. By the Middle Ages the brewhouse had become a necessity of equal importance to the kitchen in the domestic household. The responsibility for brewing ale during medieval times fell on the 'alewife'. She had to ensure that there was sufficient for the entire household, selling some on at market or at her back door to make extra money. Hell and damnation awaited any woman who gave a short measure or adulterated her brew as the intricate carvings over the choir stalls (misericord) in the choir of St Laurence, Ludlow, graphically depicts.

Throughout the fourteenth and fifteenth centuries, many more alehouses appeared which brewed and sold ale on the premises, typically a ground-floor room in a small cottage offering warmth, shelter and perhaps basic food. Today's tap house, brewpub and microbrewery are the direct descendants of these archaic establishments, following on in an ancient tradition. Brewing began to change with the Industrial Revolution, with the insatiable growth of the newly established public houses. Increasingly, the new pubs, taverns and inns found it more convenient to buy their ale from breweries. Barrels

A caricature of the dishonest alewife, who gives short measure, carried off by demons and cast into hell. A misericord in St Laurence, Ludlow.

were delivered by horse-drawn dray, serving a number of establishments in a town or outlying district. Eventually the canals, and later the railways, made it economic to deliver over larger distances, spurring the growth of national breweries. Gradually most public houses abandoned brewing ale at their premises, opting for deliveries from local, regional and then national breweries which developed and grew out of the demand fuelled by takeovers and mergers. Increasingly wealthy and profit-hungry breweries began to take over pubs and install their own tenants and managers, decreasing choice and variety in the process.

Eventually every small brewery was threatened by their larger neighbours, since fewer pubs were able to buy beer in the free market place and the majority of pubs were obliged to buy beer from the large brewery. The free trade pubs were known collectively as 'Free Houses' and they were in the minority compared to the brewery-owned tied house. As local and regional breweries came under threat from bigger concerns, the traditional process of brewing ale was also rationalised. Modern profit-orientated breweries considered cask-conditioned beer (i.e. beer brought to an optimum drinkable condition by live yeast in the barrel) unprofitable, opting for a longer-life, sterile, brewery conditioned, carbon dioxide-infused, bland and tasteless alternative.

Ultimately, pubs lost their brewhouses and their local supplies of ale and cask-conditioned beer was under threat. By the early 1970s, only four pubs in the nation brewed their own beer on site; they were the Blue Anchor in Cornwall, Old Swan (Ma Pardoe's) in Netherton, Dudley, and two from Shropshire: the Three Tuns at Bishop's Castle and All Nations at Madeley. The tradition of brewing ale at the back of the pub had almost totally disappeared and pasteurised beer was set to take over. Fortunately, the situation has changed dramatically since that time, prompted by a change of attitude towards real ale and the relentless campaigning of the consumer-led pressure group

An honest alewife, provider of ale since time immemorial, Vanessa – a modern day alewife to Sir John Savile's Household, member of the Wars of the Roses Federation.

CAMRA, real cask-conditioned ale survives as an alternative to pasteurised beer. The added bonus is the growth of local real ale breweries in the county and a resurgence of the brewpub. Since the dark days of the 1970s, the revival of brewing in the county has been little short of miraculous; at the time of writing, Shropshire can boast fifteen real ale breweries supplying the free trade: Bridgnorth Brewing Company, Corvedale, Dolphin, Hanby, Hobsons, Ironbridge, Lion's Tail, Ludlow Brewing Company, Offa's Dyke, Salopian, Six Bells, Stonehouse, Three Tuns, Woods and Worfield.

BISHOP'S CASTLE: *THE SIX BELLS*

Church Street, Bishop's Castle, SY9 5AA – 01588 630144 (pub) 01588 630930 (brewery)

Take B4385 through town, the pub is opposite St John the Baptist C of E Church. Bus services to Craven Arms and Shrewsbury. The nearest railway station is at Craven Arms.

Across the road from the parish church of St John the Baptist, this former nineteenth-century coaching inn is named after the peal of six bells, which hang in the church tower. The church is Norman in origin, substantially rebuilt during the nineteenth century, although the bells mostly date back to the eighteenth century. Bishop's Castle also has an ecclesiastical connection named after its castle (now long gone) which belonged to the Bishop of Hereford and his descendants, appointed as Marcher

The Six Bells, Bishop's Castle.

The brewery yard at
the Six Bells.

Owner and head
brewer Nev Richards
making preparations
for the next brew.

In the public bar, Six Bells.

Lords. The town has changed little from the time when Welsh drovers herded cattle, sheep and geese across the border to market. The drover route along the Kerry Ridgeway is now part of history along with the Shrewsbury turnpike and the town's own light railway, which once connected to the Shrewsbury and Hereford main line – still commemorated by the Bishop's Castle Railway Museum in the town. Despite these changes, Bishop's Castle remains largely unaltered with a sense of timeless tradition.

The Six Bells Brewery was reborn in 1997 on the site of an earlier brewery, which had closed in the early years of the twentieth century. Brews include a number of seasonal ales along with the mainstay draught beer, traditional English bitter such as Big Nev's (named after the owner Nev Richards), Cloud Nine, Marathon Bitter and Brew 10. The brewery also supplies to local free trade outlets in Shropshire and is a regular guest beer in many pubs throughout the UK.

The pub is a three-storey building similar to others in the town, with upper and lower framed windows symmetrically distributed around a single covered entrance and dormer windows in the roof. At the rear of the building is a pleasant courtyard and terrace garden which overlooks the brewery yard and there is a covered barn for smokers. On opposite sides of the main entrance are the public bar and lounge. The public bar has quarry tile floors, wooden seats and a large counter. The lounge bar has tables and chairs for diners and an intimate serving hatch. The regulars and the staff are chatty, jovial and eager to converse with a stranger.

BISHOP'S CASTLE: *THE THREE TUNS INN*

Salop Street, Bishop's Castle, SY9 5BW – 01588 638797
www.threetunsinn.co.uk

BISHOP'S CASTLE: *THREE TUNS BREWERY, JOHN ROBERTS BREWING CO. LTD*

16 Market Square, Bishop's Castle, SY9 5BN – 01588 638392
www.threetunsbrewery.co.uk

The inn is in Salop Street at the top of the town. Public car parks in Harley Jenkins Street, High Street and Station Street. Bus services to Craven Arms and Shrewsbury. Nearest railway station is at Craven Arms on the Hereford–Shrewsbury line.

Bishop's Castle stands in splendid rural isolation at the edge of the Clun Forest. The medieval pattern of streets established around the castle of motte and bailey construction survives, even if the castle does not. The town's many half-timbered buildings, most dating back to the sixteenth century, all huddle closely together on the steeply inclined streets which led to the castle mound, and at the top of the town is the Three Tuns Inn, a typical market inn, with an adjoining brewery of the same name.

The Three Tuns Inn, Bishop's Castle.

During the nineteenth century the weekly livestock market held in the streets would pack the pub to the eaves with farmers and livestock drovers, many of whom used the inn for their business transactions and a place to stay. At the annual May Fair the pub was a labour exchange, a place for local gentleman farmers to hire farm labourers for the year, the contract sealed with ale and a silver shilling. John Roberts purchased the brewery and pub in the 1880s and passed it down through three consecutive generations of the family. It was run by John's son, Erskine, and then grandson, also named John, up to the mid-1970s by which time the Three Tuns Inn was one of only four homebrew pubs left in the whole country. Its survival is testimony to the custodianship of John Roberts.

Today the inn and the brewery are separate businesses. Scottish & Newcastle Breweries now own the Three Tuns Inn while the brewery, with its Grade II listed Victorian tower, belongs to Bill Bainbridge and John Russell with Mick Leadbetter as brewery manager. The inn and the brewery stand next to each other and deserve equal mention, not least since the brewery licence was granted in 1642 and parts of the original brewhouse date back to that time, making the Three Tuns a contender for the oldest working brewery in Britain. The surviving four-storey red-brick tower built for John Roberts in 1888 is a fine example of a rural gravity-fed brewery tower. Malt and hops are winched to the top of the tower where the ingredients are mixed in a mash tun with hot liquor pumped up from the ground floor. The wort is boiled in the coppers on the next floor down, after which the hopped wort makes its way down through pipes under gravity into the fermenting vessels, and when fermented is poured into the conditioning tanks and casks.

The Three Tuns, from an early twentieth-century postcard *Exclusive, Sepiatone.* (*The Photocrom Co. Ltd, London and Tunbridge Wells*) (Author's Collection).

The sweet liquid from the mash tun (where malted flour is mixed with hot water to release sugars) 'wort', is gently boiled with hops in the copper.

Empty casks waiting to be filled.

The Three Tuns Inn has an intimate public bar with a large fireplace and wood-burning stove; the floor is quarry-tiled and authentic wooden beams are part of the structure of the room. The bar is totally separate from the dining areas with rustic wooden-backed settles, chairs and tables. In the lounge bar and dining room are handcrafted wooden stairs, banisters and window frames, and a staircase and passageway leads up to a large assembly room with a splendid wooden floor. Adjoining the assembly room is a clubroom and bar.

The classic Victorian tower brewery. Note the spent grain collected in the trailer after sparging in the mash tun (spraying with hot water to remove the last trace of sugars). The liquid sugary 'wort' flows to the copper and then, after boiling with hops, is filtered by gravity through the 'hop back' into the fermentation vessel.

BRIDGNORTH: *THE KINGS HEAD & STABLE BAR*

3 Whitburn Street, Bridgnorth, WV16 4QN – 01746 762141 and 01588 764243
www.kingsheadbridgnorth.co.uk

BRIDGNORTH BREWING CO. LTD, THE OLD BREWHOUSE

Kings Head Courtyard, Whitburn Street, Bridgnorth, WV16 4QN – 01746 762889
www.bridgnorthbrewing.com

The pub is on Whitburn Street adjoining High Street in High Town. Parking in town centre. Bus services from High Street. The Severn Valley Railway heritage line connects with national rail services at Kidderminster.

The Kings Head is a Grade II listed sixteenth-century posting inn and is one of the oldest public houses in Bridgnorth High Town. It was formerly known as the Kings Head Railway Coach House and Posting House. It was most probably

The Kings Head. The brewery yard and outdoor seating area are as attractive as the front of the building.

A postcard view of the Kings Head and St Leonard's church in the background, from a postcard published by *L. Wilding & Co., Shrewsbury Artist E.A. Phipson.* (Author's Collection)

A little-altered view one evening over a hundred years later.

rebuilt from the remains of a building destroyed by fire in 1646 when Parliamentarian forces bombarded the town. The earliest mention of the building is in 1777 and it was first licensed in 1780. In the eighteenth century, Bridgnorth became a significant turnpike crossroads and stage route. Named coaches such as 'Hibernia', 'L'Hirondelle', 'Shropshire Hero' and the 'Royal Mail' coach departed daily from outside the Crown and Kings Head, bound for Worcester, Shrewsbury, Birmingham and Cheltenham. The Kings Head jealously guarded its route known as the 'ground' against rival inns and it flourished and expanded in the heyday of the coaching era. An omnibus between Shifnal superseded the coach in later years.

The Kings Head adapted to being a popular town local after the decline of the stage and posting business, brought about by the coming of the railways, and managed to survive brewery takeovers and attempts to bring it up to date. Fortunately, the interior remained relatively unaltered structurally, although it suffered the usual superficial defacements perpetrated during the decades since the 1960s. However, it was spared the fate that befell its two high street neighbours, the Swan that had its interior gutted when it was converted into a cavernous open-plan eatery (although its splendid exterior remains), and the Crown, practically unrecognisable as a coaching inn. The Kings Head underwent a complete restoration and refurbishment in 2005. Interior oak beams (some allegedly from Wenlock Abbey) have been stripped of

Relaxing at a fireside table.

accumulated layers of black paint and have regained their former appearance. Newly painted walls refresh the separate bars and dining areas while the relaid stone flag floors and releaded front windows give the interior a light, airy feel. There are wooden settles, oak tables and chairs in each bar and open fireplaces with the delicate scent of wood smoke from each fire grate. The exterior of the building (roof, chimneys, etc.) has been restored and all the timbers are now exposed. The stable block has been converted into the Stable Bar with wisteria and hanging baskets adorning the walls. The courtyard is now a pleasant, open, umbrella-covered dining and seating area. Like most old inns, the Kings Head has a resident ghost. Supposedly friendly, the spectre manifests its presence by spontaneously switching on lights without using the light switch. Recent ghostly sightings were in the back bar, when on two occasions a figure was seen briefly sitting by the fire.

Bridgnorth's once-thriving brewery industry and countless home-brew pubs had all disappeared by the 1970s. However, the town has seen two small breweries reopen. The Bridgnorth Brewing Company (now the only surviving brewery in the town) started brewing in the courtyard of the Kings Head in 2007 on the site of a seventeenth-century brewhouse. The new brewery supplies to the free trade and the Kings Head next door. It brews a range of real ales including Old Mo, named after Bridgnorth's debauched and drunken friar (who still haunts the town), and the strong Wesgate Winter Warmer.

CHESWARDINE: *RED LION & LION'S TALE BREWERY*

High Street, Cheswardine, near Market Drayton, TF9 2RS – 01630 661234

About 2 miles along local roads from A529 Market Drayton and Hinstock road, 1 mile from the Shropshire Union (main line) Canal. Bus services to Market Drayton and Newport.

The Red Lion is the brewery tap house next door to the Lion's Tale Brewery which started brewing in March 2006. The pub sells cask-conditioned beer and bottled beer along with a wide choice of whisky. It is a true village local and is one of two pubs in High Street; the Red Lion's neighbour the Fox & Hounds stands opposite St Swithun's Church. The church dates from the thirteenth century and occupies the highest point in the village. St Swithun's is one of the oldest buildings in Cheswardine, apart from the remains of a couple of castle mounds and the manorial hall on the outskirts of the village. The village lies close to the border with Staffordshire and local amenities include a primary school, village shop and residential housing but, like many other Shropshire villages, its post office closed in 2006. The village of Cheswardine is 1 mile from the Shropshire Union Canal and the Wharf Tavern at Goldstone (see Chapter 6). The canals were once a way of life for the present landlord of the Red Lion, a former employee of British Waterways before he became a publican and brewer – prints of canal scenes hang on the walls in the bar. Landlord Jon bought the Red Lion in 1996 and has kept the charm and atmosphere of this country pub, without the distractions of jukebox, television, pool table and meals, although the pub does host a monthly quiz night. Outside, during the summer, the walls display colourful hanging baskets above a pleasant front terrace and seating area.

The Red Lion, Cheswardine.

The front bar. Note the long table on the left on which a murdered child's body was laid out in 1843.

Customers must exercise caution on
entering the front door of the pub,
in case they encounter the pub cat.

The Red Lion once belonged to the Crystal Fountain Brewery based in Market Drayton. It was bought by Marston's and later sold to the present landlord as a free house. The pub relies totally on local people as it has little or no passing trade, other than the dedicated drinker or tourist eager to experience a classic English pub. Inside are three separate front bar rooms and a back bar, served from two counters, one opening out to the front lounge and the other to the back bar. Over the bar is an impressive array of pump handle clips and a record of the guest beers served in the pub over the years. A coal-fired stove in the lounge and wood-burning stove in the front bar, stools, high-backed chairs and wooden ceiling beams decorated with horse brasses complete the scene.

In the front bar is a table on which it is reputed the body of murdered child was laid out. An inquest in 1843 established that the boy was murdered by his father; the motive was that he wanted to marry but the boy posed an obstacle. The father was found guilty and hanged for his crime at Stafford. Curiously, five years earlier in 1838 a similar

The two-and-a-half barrel capacity plant brews weekly, usually starting on a Tuesday. There are three regular brews using English hops: the ever-popular Lionbru at 4.1 per cent ABV, Blooming Blonde at 4.1 per cent ABV and Chesbrewnette at 4.5 per cent ABV. They are also available bottled and in a presentation pack sold at the counter.

child murder occurred, again a child who stood in the way of a couple's plans. Taken to a nearby lake, the child, no match for two adults, was murdered by drowning. Both assailants were arrested and trialled. The man turned King's Evidence but the woman was found guilty and hanged at Stafford.

CLEOBURY MORTIMER: *KINGS ARMS*

6 Church Street, Cleobury Mortimer, DY14 8BS – 01299 270252

The pub stands on the main thoroughfare through town. Park in the pay and display car park off St Mary's Road.

The turnpike road from Bewdley in Worcestershire, after crossing the Severn, headed west through the Wyre Forest making Cleobury Mortimer the ideal stopping point before crossing the Clee Hills on the way to Ludlow. The recently refurbished Kings Arms, leased by local brewers Hobsons, is an eighteenth-century coaching inn which lay on this route. The town of Cleobury dates back to Saxon times, but the addition of Mortimer to its name dates to shortly after the Norman Conquest (1066) when Ralph de Mortimer was appointed by William the Conqueror to subdue Edric, Earl of Shrewsbury, and his rebellion. Mortimer was granted Edric's estates, which included Cleobury, for his part in Wild Edric's downfall.

Opposite the Kings Arms is the Church of the Virgin Mary, founded by the Saxon Queen Edith. The present church dates back to the twelfth century and carries a crooked wooden spire. The pub, flanked by half-timbered and stone-built houses, is near the old post office, which has a plaque commemorating Simon Evans, Cleobury's famous writer who suffered from the effects of gas during the First World War and took the rural postal round to improve his health. A footpath between Cleobury and Stottesdon, 'The Simon Evans Way', established by the Cleobury Mortimer Footpath Association, commemorates him.

Kings Arms, Cleobury Mortimer.

A welcoming smile behind the bar, serving Hobsons award-winning mild.

Inside the Kings Arms is a central bar counter serving adjoining front rooms, separated by a wall and fireplaces with a cosy rear bar to the side. Outside is a covered seating area in the courtyard. The pub had closed prior to Hobsons making an offer to take it over. Grubby, run-down and with an assortment of social problems, the former owners were unable to find a suitable tenant to run it and, therefore, closed the premises. Concerned about the loss of one of the town's pubs, Nick Davies of Hobsons brewery approached the owners and negotiated terms to lease the property and supply his own beer. An amicable agreement was reached and Hobsons acquired what might be termed a brewery tap.

CLEOBURY MORTIMER: *HOBSONS BREWERY*

Newhouse Farm, Cleobury Mortimer, DY14 8RD – 01299 270837
www.hobsons-brewery.co.uk

Hobsons sells 9- and 18-gallon barrels and non-returnable 10 and 20-litre size polypins by telephone order, and they occasionally run brewery tours.

Hobsons is Shropshire's premier independent brewery and its range of cask-conditioned beers is sold on draught in public houses throughout Shropshire and nearby counties. Their bottle-conditioned beer sells in shops and supermarkets nationally, while Hobsons Mild is the guest beer in the Strangers' Bar at the Houses of Parliament. The Hobsons label is likely to appear in many of the free trade historic pubs of Shropshire, at beer festivals and the Ludlow Food Festival, or even in a buffet car on the preserved Severn Valley Railway – aptly named Steam No. 9 (Manor Ale). The brewery, founded in 1993, utilised salvaged second-hand plant giving the fledgling enterprise a ten- to twelve-barrel capacity. With Hobsons Best Bitter well-received, capacity increased to seventy barrels in 1995. By 2001 a new brewery was built to meet the ever-increasing demand for the popular range of cask beers: Best Bitter, Hobsons Mild (voted the best beer in Britain 2007 at the Great British Beer Festival), Town Crier and seasonal beers Old Henry, Manor Ale and Postman's Knock.

Hobsons brewery is a success story. The business has expanded and uses the latest technology and state of the art plant and, amazingly, the brewing process has changed little over time. True to the brewers' art, the ingredients used are of the highest quality and the highest level of skill and expertise are utilised to make real cask-conditioned beer, full of flavour, with a pleasant bouquet and a good head, as part of an age-old brewing tradition. Shropshire's small, independent brewers (although each brewery has its own recipes, special techniques and very different brews) have kept traditional brewing alive in the county. The basic brewing process is the same for all real ale breweries, following a number of distinct stages:

1. **Milling**
The mill rolls the malted barley (usually a blend of different types) to obtain a suitable mix of 'grist' (flour) which is then transported to a mash-tun.

2. **Mashing**
The crushed malt is mixed with hot 'liquor' (term given for hot water) in a mash tun and allowed to stand while starch converts to sugar.

3. **Running Off**
The sugary solution called 'wort' is recirculated and finally run off into a copper by spraying (sparging) with liquor until all the sugars are extracted from the malt.

4. **The Copper**
The 'wort' is boiled with hops in a copper. After boiling, the copper is 'cast' to the hopback (allowed to run through a bed of hops) and the hopped 'wort' is cooled by heat exchange or paraflow (a process of cooling the 'wort' and heating more 'liquor' for the next mash) and then pumped into the fermentation vessel.

5. **Fermentation**
The 'wort' is 'pitched' (inoculated with yeast ferments) in a vessel for five to seven days, during which time most of the sugars convert into alcohol and carbon dioxide. The yeast is then gathered and the vessel is cooled to flocculate the suspended solids.

6. **Cask Racking**
Beer is held for a few days in a conditioning tank to clear and then dropped to the racking tank for 'racking' into casks: firkins of 9 imperial gallons, kilderkins of 18 gallons or barrels of 36 gallons. The barrels are inoculated with hops and yeast to promote a secondary fermentation in the barrel.

7. **Cask-Conditioning**
The beer delivered to the pub develops its full flavour in the pub cellar under the watchful eye of the cellar-man or woman.

As Nick Davis of Hobsons demonstrates, quality ingredients are essential to good beer. Only the best quality Worcestershire hops, full of aroma and flavour, are used.

The storage tanks next to the loading bay are for malted barley. The overhead feed pipes convey ground grist to the mash tuns in another part of the brewery.

Nick Davis demonstrating the benefits of the recently installed forty-five-barrel brewhouse.

The start of the fermentation process.

The pleasant peacock-eye finishes to both the hot liquor tank and the copper.

Hobsons bottling
plant.

Casks conditioned and awaiting delivery.

CORFTON: *SUN INN*

Corfton, Craven Arms, SY7 9DF – 01584 861239

On the B4368 Craven Arms and Much Wenlock road. Bus routes to Much Wenlock, Craven Arms and Ludlow.

Shropshire's Corvedale Valley is one of the county's most beautiful and tranquil regions, at the heart of the Shropshire Hills. The area is steeped in history and folklore; nearby is the mysterious circular earthwork ramparts of Corfton Castle, its bailey under modern farm buildings. Next to it are the remains of the chapel of St Bartholomew.

The Sun Inn is a seventeenth-century inn at a crossroads on the former Much Wenlock and Craven Arms turnpike. With its back to the southern slopes of Wenlock Edge, it serves a scattered community of cottages, farms and nearby villages. The earliest mention of the Sun Inn is in county records which date back to 1613. The pub also appears in the first edition of the Ordnance Survey map of Shrewsbury, published in 1833; it is clearly marked on the turnpike route. The Sun has always been a wayside inn and as such was

The Sun Inn, Corfton.

The very tightly packed brewhouse with mash tun,
copper and fermenting vessels nestled closely together.

A selection of Corvedale Brewery bottled beers, Dark
& Delicious, Farmer Rays and Catch Me Who Can.
Also available are Normans Pride, Katie's Pride, and
Molly Morgan named after the Queen of Hunter
Valley.

obliged to keep a bed for travellers at all times to fulfil the terms of its licence. After the
coaching and posting trade declined it was relicensed as a public house by consecutive
landlords.

The Pearce family have run the pub since 1984 and re-established the brewery, named
after the Corvedale Valley. The pub serves meals prepared from fresh local produce
(including free-range eggs from the pub's own hens) with a choice of award-winning
Corvedale beers. The lounge bar has a pool table, jukebox and dartboard, and there is
a restaurant adjoining the main bar. Outside there is a patio seating area and a garden
terrace below the brewhouse. The Corvedale Brewery, established in what was the old
chicken and fire-wood shed behind the pub, brewed its first beer, Normans Pride (named
after the landlord and head brewer Norman Pearce), in 1997.

Having a quiet chat in the bar lounge.

'Queen of Hunter Valley', Australia's Molly Morgan, was born in a cottage behind the Sun Inn, registered as daughter to Margaret and David Jones (landlord of the Sun) on 31 January 1762. Molly grew up and was schooled at Diddlebury; she married an apprentice carpenter and wheelwright, William Morgan in 1785, had a son and moved to Cold Weston across the valley. In 1790 William and Molly were arrested for stealing hemp from a linen mill. William managed to escape but Molly was less fortunate and was convicted and transported to Australia. Molly managed to return to England and remarried, but was transported back after being convicted of arson – burning down her husband's house after an argument. Back in Australia she became a successful cattle farmer and mistress to a government official. However, her success was not down to honest ranching but to cattle rustling. Once more convicted, she ended up in a penal colony. Four years later she was able to obtain a parole and with a land grant opened a number of taverns in the Hunter Valley. One, the Angel Inn, became a large shanty and developed into the city of Maitland. Free-spirited and generous, Molly would have approved of a beer named after her by Corvedale Brewery, in the village where she was born.

MADELEY: *ALL NATIONS*

20 Coalport Road, Madeley, Telford, TF7 5DP – 01952 585747

Worfield Brewing Co., All Nations Brewhouse, 20 Coalport Road, Madeley –
01746 769606
www.worfieldbrewery.co.uk

Take the adjacent road opposite the entrance to the Blists Hill Victorian Village.

The All Nations was registered as a public house in 1831 under the first licensee, Christopher Baguley. The building already existed – a key stone above the doorway records the date 1789 and the initials I.R.P. (probably the date it was built and the initials of the owner). The Baguleys held the licence until the pub was finally sold to a William Harry Lewis in 1934. In the nineteenth century it was commonplace for the ownership of the pub to be passed down through the family descendants.

There are a number of theories which try to explain how the All Nations got its name. One suggests that it came from the pieces of tobacco sold in a jar called 'all nations mixture'. Another supposes that Madeley attracted visitors from all nations who came to visit the Ironbridge Gorge to experience the sights and sounds of the new industrial age. Certainly, by 1851 the All Nations Inn offered accommodation possibly to tradespeople and visitors to the area; some may well have been from overseas or from the colonies.

The All Nations was also involved in sporting activities. Madeley Town Football Club was formed at the pub in 1885 with Walter Baguley, landlord 1894–1903, captaining the side. He was a keen sportsman and also played for Ironbridge FC and Madeley Wanderers FC as well as playing for Madeley hockey team. George Baguley, landlord 1903–14, was a team member of the Madeley Airgun Club, formed in 1904.

The All Nations, Madeley.

A quiet moment of contemplation in the bar.

Ale continued to be brewed on site throughout most of the nineteenth century and through the entire twentieth century. By the early 1970s the All Nations was one of only four home-brew pubs remaining in the UK. Since that time it has reverently been referred to as 'one of the original four'. By the 1970s, the main commercial breweries forecast that traditional draught beer was dead and that there was no market for cask-conditioned ales. Ever more popular with the real ale enthusiasts, the All Nations earned a celebrity status as a place of pilgrimage for lovers of real ale and held consecutive entries each year in CAMRA's *Good Beer Guide*. However, this brewing tradition was abruptly curtailed in 2000 when the All Nations finally closed its doors to its customers and ceased brewing. The All Nations was put up for sale and remained closed for two years, but was purchased from the previous family owners and reopened in 2002, much to the relief of the community and the loyal regulars. The new owners, Jim and Linda Birtwhistle (both former teachers), refurbished the building, reinstated real fires and outside seating for smokers. They serve quality rolls and pork pies with the finest traditional ales, offer bed and breakfast accommodation and put on folk and jazz music sessions during the summer.

The cellarer's art, driving a soft spile into the shive hole on the top of a cask to allow air to enter and promote a secondary fermentation and to let carbon dioxide escape. After vigorous fermentation stops, the soft spile is replaced by a hard spile which prevents the further escape of gas, keeping a blanket pressure in the cask and giving a head on the beer as it is served.

The Worfield Brewery yard, often with a pleasant aroma escaping from the brewhouse.

The brewery in the yard of the All Nations Inn is now home to the Worfield Brewing Company (head brewer, Mike Handley), founded at the Davenport Arms, Worfield, near Bridgnorth in 1994. The brewery left Shropshire for Bromsgrove in Worcestershire for three months in 1999, when it absorbed the Red Cross Brewery facilities and then moved back again to new premises at Bridgnorth. In 2002, the brewery moved again, this time to its present location at the All Nations, incorporating the plant there to increase the capacity to ten barrels and to resume brewing house beers at the pub, as well as expanding its own range of ales. The brewery's range of beers now includes Ironbridge ales: Ironbridge Gorgeous, Coalporter and Sabrina Special. Worfield's established brands include: Dabley Ale, Dabley Gold and Coalport Dodger Mild – many of which are now readily available as guest ales in Shropshire, adjoining counties and Wales.

Mike Handley, Worfield's head brewer, casting an eye on the hopped wort as it reaches a critical stage during the boiling process in the copper.

Checking the specific gravity to calculate the strength of the brew.

SHREWSBURY: *THE DOLPHIN*

48 St Michael's Street, Shrewsbury, SY1 2EZ – 01743 350419

Take the A5191 town centre road, ½ a mile from the railway station follow Castle Forgate Street and St Michael's Street in the opposite direction from the town centre.

The Dolphin brewery opened during Christmas 2000 as a two-and-a-quarter-barrel plant which, in the summer of 2001, was increased to four-and-a-half-barrel capacity. The brewery is the tap for the Dolphin Inn. Brewing has been sporadic in recent years with occasional seasonal ales. It is, however, the intention of the landlord to continue to brew beer on occasion. The pub dates from the 1860s and stands alongside what used to be the Whitchurch turnpike (today it is the A5112 and A49 trunk road) and is built in the predominately industrial district bordering Coton Hill, north of Shrewsbury railway station. The area comprised of terraced rows and back-to-backs, some of which were church-owned. There were warehouses and factories either side of the Shrewsbury Canal and the Whitchurch to Crewe railway. The pub served the local factories and the canal, hence its nautical name, the Dolphin. The canal passed under the turnpike and ran alongside Ditherington flax mill and maltings, a Grade I listed building, which is believed to be the archetypal skyscraper and the oldest surviving iron-framed building in the world, dating from 1797. The canal was crossed by the turnpike a second time at Factory Bridge, before it ended at wharves behind the Canal Tavern in New Park Road, a short distance away from the Dolphin.

The Dolphin, Shrewsbury.

Landlord and brewer, Mark Osmond lights
the gas mantle in the lounge.

Right: Harvey the English Pointer certainly
knows where to stay warm – by the fire in
the public bar.

The Dolphin has changed a great deal since Victorian times but still serves a local
community from new housing built on the cleared sites of factories and slum dwellings,
including off-duty firefighters on their social evening from the fire station next door.
Inside there are two rooms, a comfortable public bar with warm open fireplace and
an adjoining contemporary lounge with leather sofas and another open fireplace.
Interestingly, a remnant from a previous age is a gas mantle light on the wall which
is still fully functional. The smokers' area is a well laid out, partially-covered, wooden-
decked balcony with tables and umbrellas for the summer months. Railway enthusiasts
should note that the balcony overlooks Crewe Bank signal-box on the Whitchurch to
Shrewsbury line, an ideal location to glimpse the occasional steam-hauled rail tour.

TREFONEN: *BARLEY MOW*

Chapel Lane, Trefonen, SY10 9DX – 01691 656889
www.offasdykebrewery.com

Take the Trefonen to Oswestry road south-east of Oswestry.

The village of Trefonen lies on the Oswestry to Tanat Valley road on the eastern slope of Mynydd Myfyr, part of the north–south ridge known as the Oswestry Uplands. The village is on the boundary between the Welsh Hills and the relatively flat farmland of the Shropshire plain. Offa's Dyke passes along this ridge, weaving its way through the Welsh-sounding border villages of Tyn-y-coed, Treflach and Nantmawr. The dyke follows the course of the road through the village as it descends from the hillside. The old Welsh border also followed the same route and passed through the Barley Mow Inn, dividing it between Wales and England.

The Barley Mow Inn, Trefonen.

The pool table and cosy back bar.

Happy faces behind the bar.

The Barley Mow takes its name from the stacks of barley laid out to dry at harvest time. A typical rural inn, welcoming and warm with real log fires in the public and lounge bars, it serves a fine selection of cask-conditioned beers that have travelled less than 20 yards from the Offa's Dyke Brewery next door. The public bar has a pool table and separate bar, while in the lounge is a covered well with a clear inspection cover so customers can gaze into its depths while ordering a drink. Both rooms have wooden ceiling beams. A third room adjoins the lounge and is used as a separate dining area for Wednesday evening meals with a theme, curries and steak nights with a full menu between Friday and Sunday. Local produce is used, some of which is home-grown at the owners' farm. Derek Jones bought the pub and outbuildings in 2003, and with the aid of a grant from the Redundant Building Scheme renovated them and built the brewery. Brewing started in 2007 using the former five-barrel plant bought from the defunct Thomas McGuinness Brewing Company of Rochdale, based at the Cask & Feather pub. Mr Jones was ably helped by John Edwards, who supervised the installation, and brewer Alan McKenzie who had used the plant for eighteen years previously.

The clock tower
of Offa's Dyke
brewhouse.

The Offa's Dyke Brewery offers a large selection of cask-conditioned beer:
Harvest Moon, a dark mild; Harvest Gold, a light bitter; Barley Blonde, a
cask lager; Thirst Brew, a premium bitter and Grim Reaper, a strong porter
affectionately known as 'Trefonen Guinness'.

WISTANSTOW: *THE PLOUGH INN*

Wistanstow, Craven Arms, SY7 8DG – 01588 673251
www.ploughwistanstow.co.uk

WISTANSTOW: *THE WOOD BREWERY LTD*

Wistanstow, Craven Arms, SY7 8DG – 01588 672523
www.woodbrewery.co.uk

Take the A489 turn from the A49 Shrewsbury and Craven Arms road and turn right immediately after passing under the railway bridge. After about ⅓ mile, the pub and brewery are on your right with a large car park. Craven Arms is the nearest railway station. Bus route Ludlow, Craven Arms and Shrewsbury.

Situated on the main street of this quiet Shropshire village, the Plough Inn is the brewery tap for Wood's Brewery located next door. A traditional Shropshire village pub, the front of the building stands out onto a little-used country road, actually a former Roman road. On the opposite side is a large manorial farmhouse. Not unlike many other pubs of its type, the Plough may well have been a terrace of cottages gradually combined together to form one larger pub.

The Plough Inn, Wistanstow.

The bar at the Plough is the ideal spot for walkers to stop for a bite to eat, and for a pint. It is a short distance from the Marches Way, the Shropshire Way and is at the centre of the Shropshire Hills Area of Outstanding Natural Beauty.

A selection of Wood's bottled beers.

A modern family restaurant extension has been added with an entrance hallway and disabled access. The external appearance of the original building remains unaltered with its dog-friendly snug bar and games room, heated throughout with a wood-burning stove in the main bar, very warm and welcoming on a winter's day.

In summer months the patio and beer garden are a pleasant retreat for the beer-drinker, away from the lunchtime and evening diners, a place to enjoy the rural charm of the area and perhaps smell the pleasant aroma of barley grist from the brewery. The pleasure of simple home-cooked food, made from local produce, is also an experience too good to miss. The pub attracts a varied clientele and is a favourite watering hole for tourists, locals and beer buffs alike. It is also popular with walkers exploring the Shropshire Hills and visitors to the village, Holy Trinity Church and the impressive black and white-timbered village hall, built by workers from Grove Estate in the 1920s. The snug bar in the Plough is the drinkers' retreat adjoining the games and pool room which hosts the Corvedale and Wood's Brewery darts final. The pub has a Wi-Fi connection for laptop users and business clientele.

Inside the brewery, the mash tun is used for separating sugars from malted barley 'grist' by adding liquor (warm water). The warm sweet 'wort' that is produced is then pumped to the copper for boiling with hops.

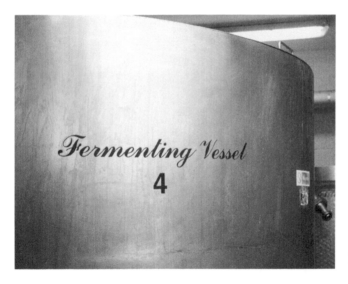

The fermentation vessel: the heart of the brewery and where the hopped wort is converted by the action of yeast into beer and carbon dioxide.

   The brewery, founded in a stable block next to the pub in 1980 by Basil Wood and helped by sons Anthony and Edward, has expanded to twice its original size. The small stable buildings now accommodate an enlarged brewery and offices. Wood's range of beers is increasingly popular in Shropshire, Wales and the Midlands with favourites like Parish Bitter, Special Bitter, Shropshire Lad and Wood's Wonderful the mainstays, along with an assortment of seasonal ales conditioned in the cask or sold bottled.

TWO

The Local

The 'local' provides a very special service: that of a place to hold a gathering and a venue for sports activities, pigeon racing and pub games. It is in these pubs that the county's football and cricket teams are based, darts leagues and local societies meet. Although locals are as old as pubs themselves, the word 'local' is more commonly associated with the public house which came into existence with the 1830 Duke of Wellington Beer Act.

As a result of low duties on gin, the uncontrolled growth of gin houses in all the major industrial centres in Britain had brought about a scourge of public drunkenness. The government responded by introducing a new category of licensed premises, permitted to sell less alcoholic beer, but no spirits or fortified wines. The act allowed any householder on payment of two guineas to brew beer or cider at home and sell it during specified hours. This proved to be an extremely popular piece of legislation. Within a few years, the number of public houses exceeded 40,000 and every county in England was affected by a rapid increase in the number of its pubs. With so many new establishments in the county, literally everyone in Shropshire had a local.

During the nineteenth and twentieth centuries, town and village locals were largely profitable concerns providing a focus for the community. Many are no longer profitable, serving only a small number of customers and, with scant takings, they are increasingly under threat of closure. The county still has many examples of town and village locals but with a new topical title that describes them –'community pub'. The pubs listed in this chapter are divided into town and village, starting with towns. A cautionary note for the benefit of readers wishing to visit any of these pubs mentioned here: locals are the least likely to have regular opening periods. Anyone intending to visit an unfamiliar local is strongly advised to telephone first to ascertain times of opening and if the pub is still trading.

The epitome of a local – the Fox inn, Oswestry.

The Town Local

BRIDGNORTH: *BELL & TALBOT*

2 Salop Road, Bridgnorth, WV16 4QU – 01746 763233
www.odleyinns.co.uk

The pub is just off the traffic island on Salop Street High Town. Use town centre car parks near supermarket.

The Bell & Talbot is a former nineteenth-century coaching inn, close to the old tollhouse which guarded the stage routes from Much Wenlock and Ludlow. The pub is part of a terraced row of houses and is a popular evening drinking establishment with two adjoining bar rooms leading to a conservatory and beer garden at the rear. A separate and more intimate public bar – home to the local quiz team – is at the front of the building, with a wooden bar counter built partly from railway sleepers,

The origin of the pub's name is not certain but it may be a combination of two common pub names: 'The Bell' after a bell from a nearby church and 'Talbot' after a hunting dog or the family name of the Earl of Shrewsbury.

In the main bar, an assortment of records and musical instruments are hung from the ceiling, which confirms the pub is a popular Friday and Sunday venue for live music, featuring local bands and vocalists. At one time the Bell & Talbot was also a wet-fish

shop but it is now a true drinking pub. The pub serves bar meals on Thursdays and Sunday evenings. True to its coaching inn heritage, it also offers accommodation with en suite rooms and holds a spring and autumn beer festival. The pub belongs to a small group of pubs, Odley Inns Limited (see also Coach and Horses, Shrewsbury Chapter 3).

The Bell & Talbot, Bridgnorth.

The front bar, partially made of railway sleepers.

Landlord Guy Gibson does the honours.

BRIDGNORTH: *THE FRIARS INN*

3 St Mary's Street, Bridgnorth, WV16 4DW – 01746 762396

The pub is located in Central Court off St Mary's Street and the High Street adjacent to the Town Hall.

Friars were clergymen with no ties to a monastery or a particular parish; they lived among the people in the towns and cities and, with no visible means of support, they often begged to survive. They first appeared in Britain in the thirteenth century, unlike the pub named after them which dates back to the nineteenth century and started out as a posting stable. The friars of the Middle Ages were well-liked, more so than their ecclesiastical brethren, monks and priests, who had something of a reputation for being unpious and debauched. Today's Friars Inn is also well liked by its visitors and regulars. Originally called the Hen and Chickens, it has no connection with medieval friars, other than its pub sign.

The artist who painted the pub sign used the retired footballer Norman Deeley as his inspiration. Deeley spent fifteen years with Wolverhampton Wanderers from 1952 to 1967 and contributed to two league titles and the FA Cup in 1960. He was capped twice for England.

The well tucked-away Friars Inn.

Landlady Joanne Goddard meeting and greeting.

The Friars from the Central Courtyard shopping area.

First licensed in 1828 as a posting house, the Friars Inn was once a brewery, cider house and blacksmiths. It is reached from a covered passageway from St Mary's Street or by the Central Court shopping area, with its small shops and stalls. The pub is small and intimate. Outside chairs provide a comfortable retreat for smokers and, in the summer months, hanging baskets ablaze with colour adorn the courtyard. Inside, there is a single large counter with plenty of standing room and dining areas on both sides. As a free house, the pub offers a variety of real ales and guest beers, bed and breakfast accommodation including traditional breakfasts and a quick, efficient service to diners at lunchtime and early evening.

CLEOBURY MORTIMER: *ROYAL FOUNTAIN INN*

Church Street, Cleobury Mortimer, DY14 8BS – 01299 270177

On the main road through the town centre. On-road car parking and nearby car park. Bus route from Ludlow to Kidderminster.

The Royal Fountain Inn, formerly the Fountain Inn, consists of three late eighteenth-century cottages combined together, once separate shops, a grocer and tea merchant with the original pub in between. It was landlord Joseph Edwards (1865–78) who prefixed 'Royal' to the name of the pub in an attempt to make it sound more appealing to customers. The pub entrance from the street is between the no-longer used lounge door and carriage arch. The first licensee was William Williams, holding a full alehouse licence in 1837. The original pub was then much smaller an area, no larger than 15 sq ft and the outbuildings were used as stables and a brewhouse.

The Royal Fountain Inn, Cleobury Mortimer.

The comfortable settee and warm fireplace in the bar.

Beer delivery at the Royal Fountain from the Three
Tuns Brewery, Bishop's Castle.

Running a pub was not always an entirely profitable occupation, especially when
there was a large family to look after. Often a licensee had to have another profession
to make ends meet. Landlady Elizabeth Williams (1839–53) was a grocer and landlord
Thomas Breakwell (1853–65) was a shoemaker. By the end of the nineteenth century,
the pub had two smoke rooms, a bar and taproom, four bedrooms and stabling for
fourteen horses. Today the Grade II listed Royal Fountain Inn has a large bar area and a
separate dining room. In the bar is a large inglenook fireplace with a wood burner. The
fireplace and some existing old beams are part of the original pub and the bow windows
are a reminder of the shop fronts. The beer garden and smokers' patio area overlooks a
small brook, a tributary of the nearby River Rea.

CLUN: *SUN INN*

10 High Street, Clun, Craven Arms, SY7 8JB – 01588 640559
www.thesunatclun.co.uk

Located on the B4368, High street. Bus service to Craven Arms and Bishop's Castle.

> Clunton and Clunbury
> Clungunford and Clun,
> Are the quietest places
> Under the sun
>
> A.E. Housman, *A Shropshire Lad*, 1896

Clun may turn out to be an even quieter place under the sun, now that this historic pub has just closed (hopefully only temporarily). The Sun called last orders on 3 January 2009, tenants Graham and Fiona Didlick and four staff losing their livelihood, all victims of the deepening recession, diminishing trade, increased overheads and high rents. In stark contrast, some of Shropshire's older established free houses in similar rural areas are proving to be more resilient economically. The Sun is one of Shropshire's finest historic pubs and rightfully deserves mention here while the owners try to rescue it as a pub and a business.

The Sun at Clun.

The public bar.

Victorian beer engine and hand pulls in the lounge bar.

While it was open, this Grade II listed fifteenth-century inn was a place for visitors to relax with a pint and enjoy a meal served in the bar or adjoining restaurant. It is a pub full of old world charm with a traditional public bar, warmed during the winter by an inglenook fireplace, with wooden floors and white walls and ceilings in between original oak timbers. The lounge bar and separate restaurant are served from a counter fitted out with genuine Victorian hand pulls. Also in the lounge is an unusual and rare wall decoration, preserved behind clear plastic, part of coverings that once covered all the walls in the room. Another interesting feature is the fire mark found at various locations throughout the pub, the symbol of the sun, which gives light, heat and vitality to all things and is an age-old symbol for an inn. Outside, the white-painted rendered walls hide the cruck beam construction of the gables, although a third cruck is exposed in the bar inside. Small windows glazed with panes of distorted glass look out onto the High Street and behind the building is the mandatory covered smoking area.

LUDLOW: *THE CHURCH INN*

The Buttercross, Ludlow, SY8 1AW – 01584 872174
www.thechurchinn.com

The pub is behind the Buttercross in the centre of Ludlow. Park in nearby pay and display car park off Castle Street. Local bus routes Shrewsbury, Kidderminster, Worcester and Hereford. Railway station ¼ mile from the pub.

The Church Inn hides behind Butter Cross Market Hall (built 1743), between College Street and a narrow passage called Church Calends which leads to the south porch of the parish church of St Laurence. The church was originally dedicated to the Blessed Apostles Philip and James, as well as St Laurence. By the mid-thirteenth century, the dedication was just to St Laurence. The east window of the church depicts his martyrdom, burnt alive on a gridiron. Parts of the inn date back to the fourteenth century, before the Black Death, when the inn was called the 'Cross Keys'. Crossed keys represented the keys to heaven and the symbol of the pope. At the time the pub belonged to the Palmers' Guild, founded in Ludlow in about 1250. Members of the guild paid fees for chaplains to hold masses and pray for the members' souls while they were alive and after death. The chaplains lived in the college buildings opposite the west door, conveniently close to the inn. At the Reformation in 1551, the guild's assets were surrendered to the Crown and the inn passed to Ludlow Corporation.

The Church Inn, Ludlow.

Welcoming smiles from the pulpit.

Still known as the Cross Keys, parts of the inn were used at various times by a barber-surgeon, blacksmith and saddler. It was then later known as the 'Wine Tavern near the Cross'. During the middle part of the nineteenth century, Ambrose Grounds, a former mayor of Ludlow, used the property as a chemist's shop. In the later part of the nineteenth century the pub was called 'John Wollaston's Wine Vaults'. Wollaston sold it on to Cheltenham Original Brewery Co., who renamed it Exchange Vaults. Burton upon Trent brewers Ind Coope bought the pub in 1901, selling it to Mitchell & Butlers in 1954. In the early 1970s the pub was renamed the 'Gaiety Inn', changing to the more aptly named Church Inn by 1979.

The Church Inn regularly appears in the CAMRA *Good Beer Guide* and has an enviable reputation as a real ale pub which is always busy and ever popular. A true inn, it offers en suite accommodation and meals served in a separate dining area. There are two comfortable bars with ample seating and an upstairs lounge. During summer evenings the seating extends outside, under the arches of the Butter Cross. Garlands of hops hang from the ceilings and pictures of church buildings line the walls, reminding customers of the Church Inn's ecclesiastical connection. The rear bar has a cosy alcove, a real fireplace and comfortable seating; the perfect place to read a newspaper and enjoy a pint.

MUCH WENLOCK: *THE GEORGE & DRAGON INN*

2 High Street, Much Wenlock, TF13 6AA – 01952 727 312

Nearest car park off St Mary's Road. Local bus service between Bridgnorth and Shrewsbury.

The George & Dragon is a popular local in this picturesque unspoilt market town. A former coaching inn, parts of the pub probably date back to the early sixteenth century. The town of Much Wenlock lies on the north-east slopes of the Wenlock Edge escarpment, a magnet for walkers and geologists. The town is famous for the ruins of its priory and for the Festival at the Edge, the biggest storytelling festival in the country. It is also famous for the Wenlock Olympic Games – held annually in July since 1850. The games inspired the modern Olympic movement, the legacy of Dr William Penny-Brookes (1809–95) who introduced physical education into British schools for the 'promotion of moral, physical and intellectual improvement.'

The George & Dragon, Much Wenlock.

In the bar.

The entrance to the George & Dragon is from the High Street, through a central door flanked by three large windows. Inside is an oblong serving counter to one corner. Tall, high-backed wooden settles with soft cushions circle the room and there are genuine oak ceiling beams from which a variety of whisky water jugs hang. In the bar there are well-polished black and terracotta quarry floor tiles and a wooden floored area next to the bar. A hallway leads to two separate intimate dining rooms. Next to an interesting panel door there is an alcove with old photographs showing scenes from the former brewery yard. The dining rooms are similarly adorned with over 200 jugs hanging from the ceiling beams, above tables set out for diners. Walls are painted off-white with paintings depicting the legend of George and the dragon, England's patron saint.

The beam over the fireplace in the bar has carved – in no particular order – initials of former licensees, all members of the Yates family, who held the licence between 1835 and 1958. The first recorded owner was a Thomas Bowdler (1714), probably the innkeeper. The first licensee was George Yates in 1835 and the current licensee is Angela Gray who took over the pub at the end of 2006. The George & Dragon has a dog-friendly bar but the owner and the dog must be wary, because one of the four resident ghosts is a dog who resides in the cellar and whose eerie bark can be heard in the night. The other spectres manifest themselves from time to time or cause glasses to inexplicably fall from tables and shatter – most recently witnessed when a rock band played at the pub.

A trusting dragon joins St George for a light snack and tankard of ale, from wall paintings in the dining rooms of indeterminate age.

The dragon lays slain, as St George takes refreshment after the battle in the gruelling sun.

The perfect drinking pose in the best spot after the bar counter.

NEWPORT: *THE NEW INN*

2 Stafford Road, Newport, TF10 7LX – 01952 814729

Take Stafford Street from High Street. The pub is at the traffic lights between Stafford Road and Audley Road.

Newport is a market town established during the reign of Henry I with a typical wide main street and narrow streets radiating from an open market square. The town developed along Norman burgage plots – essentially strips of land extending from the centre. The town was relatively prosperous during medieval times, trading in fish (caught in Aqualate Mere, Staffordshire), leather and wool. Many early medieval buildings were destroyed in the great fire of 1665 and the town was rebuilt extensively during the Georgian and Regency periods. At the height of the Industrial Revolution, Newport remained a rural market town served by the Shrewsbury & Newport Canal, turnpikes and eventually the railway in 1849.

The New Inn replaced an earlier inn, the Queens Head, that once stood at the opposite side of the Stafford Road in Watery Lane (now Water Lane) leading down to the canal, which was destroyed in a fire that consumed the tannery in Tan Bank. The Queens Head lay on a drove route, which extended from the Welsh border into Staffordshire and then through the length of the country to London. The road between Newport and Stafford was turnpiked in 1763 and The New Inn, built a year before, took advantage of the increase in passing trade. The pub offered accommodation, stabling and a wheelwrights

The New Inn, Newport.

At the service counter.

In the lounge.

shop and there was a blacksmith's forge at the corner of Marsh Lane (now Audley Road). The New Inn belonged to Edwin Humphreys who bought land straddling the turnpike from a local baker, John Podmore. The land comprised a walled garden and orchard. A Civic Pride Award for Newport in Bloom was awarded in 2002 for parts of the restored garden.

The New Inn has become more of a back street local since the Stafford road was diverted out of the town. Resigned to a more peaceful existence, it is now a popular town local. The pub has retained its individual bar rooms. In the front bar there is a wood-burning stove, lots of ceiling beams and a frosted, engraved window, quarry tile floors and high-backed chairs. The public bar has a dartboard and trophies with prize cups on the mantlepiece; another back bar has a pool table. A passageway leads to a patio and small beer garden for smokers. The counter in the passageway has a glazed screen and serves the front and back bars.

The pigeons safely in their baskets and ready to depart to the release point. The clocks are synchronised and set for a race, with members of the Newport (Salop) North Road Invitation Flying Club (NRIFC) who meet every Friday at the New Inn between April and September and Saturdays after a race to work out velocities.

OSWESTRY: *THE FOX INN*

Church Street, Oswestry, SY11 25U – 01691 679669

Take Church Street south from the Cross (B5069) in the town. Car parking is at Festival Square and Central car park. Bus station in Station Road opposite Cambrian Visitor Centre ,while the nearest railway station is at Gobowen.

From the street, the Fox Inn looks small and unimposing but the pub extends some distance rearwards. The entrance passageway and narrow courtyard behind the pub emerges in a much wider yard in front of a stage and a rustic heated smokers' shelter – complete with leather Chesterfield. The yard has umbrella-covered tables for barbecues during summer months and regular live music. The front of the pub appears asymmetric and it is possible that part of the side was removed. Isaac Watkin, in his book *Oswestry with an account of its old houses, shops, etc and some of their occupants* (1920), writes how a Victorian gentleman walked into the low-projecting gable of the inn and damaged his silk hat. The threat of the law prompted Richard Smale, then landlord, to remove or alter the gable.

The Fox Inn, Oswestry – especially inviting at night time.

A welcoming smile at the bar.

Relaxing in the lounge bar.

The front bar has two entrances: a cramped street-side doorway and a side entrance from the passageway – by way of the second bar room. The front bar is small and intimate and it is the only serving counter for the pub. The second bar room has a large inglenook fireplace on the far wall, low ceilings and quarry tile floors. Moving further back through the pub is a third room with a higher ceiling and an impressive high settle with turned newel posts supporting a wooden canopy. Further back is the final smaller room, home to the Royal Naval Association of Oswestry with a small fireplace and appropriate naval emblems and pictures on the walls. A doorway connects this final room to the outside yard.

Looking back from the long courtyard.

WHITCHURCH: *OLD TOWN HALL VAULTS*

St Mary's Street, Whitchurch, SY13 1QU – 01948 662251

Use town centre car parks. The pub is just off the High Street before the junction with Green End, half a mile from the railway station. Bus routes to Ellesmere, Wem, Market Drayton, and out of the county to Wrexham, Nantwich and Chester.

Whitchurch, founded by the Romans between AD 52 and 70, grew over the centuries into a moderately sized town. The name for the town comes from 'white church' and refers to a Norman white stone church, St Alkmund's, which was rebuilt entirely in 1712 in sandstone. The town has a fair selection of pubs, although a number have recently closed and others are under a stay of execution. Many served as coaching inns in the heyday of the nineteenth-century posting era, but most are now town centre locals. The Old Town Vaults, built in about 1790, is a traditional market tavern and a local. The pub is famous as the birthplace of composer Sir Edward German (1862–1936).

Born German Edward Jones, the second of five children, he was taught to play the piano and organ by his father – who was a church organist. German taught himself the violin and composition. He sang in the church choir and, when a teenager, formed a quintet with his sister and friends. Accepted into the Royal Academy of Music he

continued to study the violin and changed his name to Edward German. By 1884, the academy appointed him as a violin instructor during which time he composed a light opera, *The Two Poets*, and his first symphony. In 1888, German became conductor and musical director at the Globe Theatre, writing music for productions such as *Richard III* (1889), Henry Irving's version of *Henry VIII* (1892) and *Nell Gwynn* (1900). When Arthur Sullivan (of Gilbert and Sullivan fame) died in 1900, German took a commission to finish Sullivan's *The Emerald Isle* with Basil Hood as librettist. Its success prompted German to write another comic opera, *Merrie England*, in 1902, again in partnership with Basil Hood. German's next successful opera was *Tom Jones* in 1907. In 1911, he wrote the music score for *Henry VIII* movie. A celebrated conductor and one of the first composers to conduct his own music for a gramophone recording, he received a

Old Town Hall Vaults, Whitchurch.

knighthood in 1928 and the Royal Philharmonic Society's gold medal in 1934. German died in 1936, at the age of seventy-four, largely forgotten in his hometown but known to the clientele of the Old Town Vaults and its occasional celebrity visitors.

Sir Edward would have probably been quite comfortable in the present-day pub since it has changed little since his day. There is a separately partitioned dining and function room leading off from the side of the main bar. A large wooden counter serves the main bar room and rear snug, with a large selection of real ales on tap. A Welsh flag drapes from the ceiling and a large portrait of Sir Edward German hangs above the fireplace. Also in the main bar are framed newspaper cuttings with stories about the tavern. One cutting refers to an incident when the fire brigade was called to the pub to put out a chimney blaze while locals, undisturbed, continued drinking at the bar. Another cutting refers to 1940s rationing which limited beer to 1½ pints per night. The pub has a Grade II listed toilet outside in the yard and three unusual ghosts known as Albert, Martha and a ghostly cat called Topsy.

Jack Faulkner, thirty years a local at the Old Town Vaults, sits below a portrait of composer Sir Edward German.

The Village Local

Unfortunately, many village pubs are under threat of closure and many that close are demolished and redeveloped. In a town, the loss of one pub to a community might not raise a concern provided others remain open, but the closure of a village local has a far greater impact on a community, especially if it is the only pub in the village. Many Shropshire villages have now lost their last pub and as more are threatened, the argument for preserving the pub as a focus for the community is gaining strength. More and more people are voicing their objections, protesting and campaigning against the loss of their village local(s).

It is not always a simple case of economics, profit and loss or the balance book which decides the fate of a pub; a developer has to make a strong case for demolishing a village pub to make way for rural housing development, and the decision process is subject to public scrutiny. His task, however, is made easier when the pub in question has no redeeming historical features or unique character sufficient to mitigate demolition. English Heritage might give a favourable report at a planning meeting or an enquiry and possibly list the building if it meets their criteria, but often a pub and especially a local is deemed to be 'of no historical importance'.

The closure of the Railway Inn at Pontesbury is a typical example. The building was subject to a planning review and assessed by English Heritage in 1999, who confirmed that the pub appeared to date from the eighteenth century, but added, '... the fenestration has been altered and the interior opened up with current fittings being of no historic interest.' They added, 'its architectural interest is diminished by various additions and therefore does not posses sufficient architectural or historic interest to merit listing the building.' The application to demolish the pub and construct dwellings was given in 2004, despite thirty-three protest letters and a petition signed by 400 residents of Pontesbury who believed the Railway Inn was capable of being refurbished.

Although a village pub might come under threat, its chances of survival are greater if it is of historic interest, especially if English Heritage lists the buildings. Another recent closure of a listed pub is the Sun at Clun. Although closed as this book goes to press, it will be of interest to see what part this pub's historic credentials play in the argument to keep it open. However, it might close as a pub if Shropshire County Council grants a change of use, but because it is a listed building it is unlikely to be demolished.

ALVELEY: *THE THREE HORSESHOES*

Church Street, Alveley Village, WV15 6NB – 01746 780642

Leave the A442 Kidderminster–Bridgnorth road by Daddlebrook Road, head for the post office at the top of the bank and the pub is on your right, with the car park at rear. Bus routes between Kidderminster and Bridgnorth. Railway at Severn Valley Railway, Country Halt and Severn Valley Country Park (1½ miles on foot).

Alveley's parish church, St Mary's, was built in 1140 to replace an earlier Saxon church. A stone cross by the Norman entrance is the only surviving feature of the earlier building. Inside is a badly damaged and faded fourteenth-century mural of the Seven Deadly Sins and monuments of the Lee family, removed from the chapel at Coton Hall when its roof collapsed in 1878. An American descendant of the family was Robert E. Lee, the famous Confederate general. St Mary's in medieval times dominated the life of the parish and Christian festivals, baptism, marriage, funerals, secular plays and pageants occasioned drinking and feasting by all. These events, known as 'church ales', were not greatly different from today's church fête, though the consumption of ale was the principal activity in former times. 'Church ales' were popular with everyone, especially with the clergy since they raised money for the church. The Three Horseshoes (built in 1406) was in all probability a church alehouse – traditionally built beside the parish church it played a part in the 'church ale'. The churchwardens commissioned the brewing of ale at the Three Horseshoes. Stronger ales were brewed periodically, especially for Christmas, All Saints' Day, Whitsun with 'bride ale' for wedding days from which the word bridal comes. Brewing continued even after the 'church ale' was banned during the Reformation. It was considered papist, too rowdy and irreverent an activity for the new puritanical church. The Three Horseshoes survived as a secular brewhouse providing rooms for drinking and lodging. Later it was registered as an inn. By the nineteenth century the inn had increased in size and was able to provide five upstairs rooms, three downstairs rooms and stabling for four horses.

The Three Horseshoes, Alverley.

In the bar.

The Wyre Forest coal seam extends under both banks of the River Severn and by the 1930s, mine workings had passed under the Severn from the nearby village of Highley. In 1935, a new mineshaft was sunk to the old workings from Alveley to modernise the existing colliery and improve productivity. Production from Alveley colliery started in 1937 and ended when the mine closed in 1969. A ropeway across the river conveyed mined coal to the washers and sidings on the Severn Valley Railway. Most of the mine's output ended up in the furnaces of Buildwas and Stourport power stations. Miners eager to quench their thirst after hard and dusty shifts at the coalface often frequented the Three Horseshoes, along with other pubs in the locality. During that time there was a pub for every 400 people from a population of 2,000 villagers. The colliery spoil heaps are landscaped into the Severn Valley Country Park with water meadows and woodland, home to a wide variety of wildlife. The Severn Way, Jack Mytton Way and Mercian Cycle route 45 pass nearby.

The Three Horseshoes, now a popular village local, offers food and hospitality to regulars and visitors to the country park. It boasts a veranda smoking area, beer garden and large car park. Some alterations, especially the curious rendering of the chimney, detract from and hide the older building. The interior on the other hand is more in keeping with the seventeenth century. In the bar are numerous wooden beams and a large inglenook fireplace, plenty of seating and a separate raised area for diners.

ASH MAGNA: *WHITE LION*

Church Lane, Ash Magna, SY13 4DR – 01948 663153

In the heart of the village, 2 miles south-east of Whitchurch, take Ash Road from A525 Nantwich Road.

Ash is a scattered Shropshire village with two distinct parts: Saxon-named Ash Magna and Ash Parva, which once belonged to the manor of Whitchuch (known then as Westune). The surrounding countryside area is predominantly flat farmland. Nearby is Brown Moss, a nature reserve created to protect plants which grow in waterlogged habitats. An RAF bomber-training unit took advantage of the flat terrain at nearby Prees Heath (Tilstock) with hundreds of acres of land used to accommodate the Second World War aerodrome. Many buildings from that time have survived; hangars converted to grain stores, three concrete runways, dispersal areas, bomb pens, barracks and the control tower. Part of the airfield is still operational for agricultural flying and parachuting.

Ash Magna has some half-timbered houses and Ash Hall is a Queen Anne-style country house and a working farm. The parish church, Christ Church, is built entirely in red brick and is almost half-a-mile outside the village. Like many other villages in Shropshire, Ash has lost its school, amenity store and post office. Fortunately it still has its pub, the White Lion, which stands to the side of a small square that used to be the playground for the local school.

White Lion, Ash Magna.

The public bar, with landlord
Roger Bentley presiding.

The public bar fireplace.

The White Lion's public bar and lounge are on opposite sides of the front main entrance.
The public bar has a quarry tile floor and single wooden bar counter with seating area
around a fireplace and a clock over the mantlepiece. On the walls there are old photographs,
prints and a dart board. There is also an assortment of bric-a-brac throughout the room.
The lounge room to the right of the main entrance has cushioned seating and tables for
diners. Home cooked food is available from a menu which includes special German dishes,
prepared by the German-born wife of landlord Roger Bentley.

The pub's new sign – spot landlord Roger Bentley in the bottom left-hand corner.

Creator of Ogri, a tough cartoon biker with wings protruding from his helmet, cartoonist and illustrator for *Bike* magazine, Paul Sample, stands below another one of his creations: the White Lion pub sign.

CLEE HILL VILLAGE: *THE KREMLIN*

Clee Hill, SY8 3NB – 01584 890950

Take the A4117 Ludlow Road over the Clee Hills and turn onto an unnamed road from Clee Hill High Street. Continue uphill towards the radio mast, the pub is signposted.

> 'From Clee to heaven the beacon burns . . .'
>
> A.E. Housman, *A Shropshire Lad*, 1896

The Kremlin has been a pub for just over a hundred years, a relative newcomer to Shropshire's list of historic pubs, but like all pubs it makes its own history. It was formerly the quarry master's house next to a large stone quarry. Minerals dug from Clee Hill and limestone, coal, clay, ironstone and dolerite were once transported from the quarry face by waggons worked over a series of inclined planes, shunted by locomotives to the railhead and than trans-shipped along the Ludlow & Clee Hill line to a rail junction at Ludlow. Opened in 1864, the line worked by the GWR and L&NW Joint Railway closed in sections between 1960 and 1962. The old railway ran along part of the dirt track road below the pub and a stile crosses over a fence from it into a field directly below the pub. The Kremlin, originally called the Craven Arms, still caters for quarry workers and local farmers. Set on common land with its own turnout rights for sheep grazing – a right that came with the tenure – it stands on Titterstone Clee, the highest ground directly west of the Urals in Russia, close to a radio mast, a few grey rendered houses and squat, windswept trees.

The Kremlin, Clee Hill, from the old railway trackbed.

The Kremlin's isolated
hillside aspect.

In the bar.

During the 1980s the pub was renamed the Kremlin because Radio Moscow could
be heard coming from the jukebox when no music was playing, an eerie phenomenon
caused by extraneous radio signals beamed off the radio mast on top of the hill. Russian
was also heard on the telephone and the television. The radio interference stopped when
the nearby radio mast was relocated. The Kremlin is an honest, no-nonsense pub where
the regulars play darts, dominoes and quoits and the beer is excellent. The pub caters
for many summer visitors from Birmingham and the Black Country who come to take
in the magnificent views encompassing seven counties. It is the second highest pub in
England, at 1,400ft, after the Tan Hill Inn in the Pennines. A footpath from the pub car
park leads further up the hill through derelict quarry workings and up to a huge flooded
quarry, surrounded by high cliffs and spoil mounds, home to nesting peregrine falcons.
In addition to the friendly locals, the pub attracts birdwatchers, hikers and walkers and
it is a welcoming refuge in bad weather when the hills appear bleak and sparse. J.R.R.
Tolkien visited the Clee Hills frequently while travelling through Shropshire and the
Marches from Birmingham, prompting some people, including the Kremlin's locals, to
suggest that the Shire in *Lord of the Rings* is inspired by the Clee Hills area, not difficult
to believe on a fine day, although it might be more appropriate to imagine the hills and
quarries as Mordor on the bleakest of days.

COALBROOKDALE: *COALBROOKDALE INN*

12 Wellington Road, Coalbrookdale, TF8 7DX – 01952 433953
www.coalbrookdaleinn.co.uk

Turn into Dale Road from the mini-island at Ironbidge and follow signs for the Coalbrookdale Museums. The Coalbrookdale Inn is in Wellington Road between the traffic lights opposite the Museum of Iron. There is limited parking.

The Coalbrookdale Inn takes its name from the surrounding dale at the heart of a complex of museums and historic buildings, part of the Ironbridge Gorge World Heritage Site. It is opposite the Museum of Iron, Abraham Darby's Iron Furnace, the Museum Library, Ironbridge Institute and Enginuity (an interactive engineering and technology attraction). The inn is a Grade II listed building, built between 1830 and 1840, and was first licensed in 1843 to serve beer to thirsty ironworkers and offer accommodation to commercial visitors to Coalbrookdale Iron Works.

During the eighteenth and nineteenth centuries, Coalbrookdale – especially where the inn stands – was an extremely busy, noisy and dirty place with the night sky illuminated by the glow of furnaces and the days blighted by billowing smoke. Huge quantities of coke and iron ore were moved and the noise of steam engines working flat out could be heard day and night. The ironworks at Coalbrookdale grew from a plentiful supply of raw materials from the area: coal, iron, clay, and lime with an abundance of flowing water from local brooks used to turn watermills and supply cooling ponds. Nearby, the River Severn served as the main arterial route for the transportation of iron goods. However, by the end of the nineteenth century, the iron industry went into gradual decline and by the 1960s there was widespread dereliction and loss of economy.

Coalbrookdale Inn, Coalbrookdale.

The main bar, complete with early-evening regulars.

The revival came when the whole area was designated a World Heritage Site. The new-found status for the area reflected on the fortunes of the Coalbrookdale Inn and it now serves a different clientele, the tourist. The pub has many unique and historical features. 'The Dale' as its regulars call it, is lively and well frequented, offering real ale, meals and B&B accommodation. The inn has an impressive brick frontage with leaded glass windows and an imposing main entrance, reached by a symmetrical stairway. During the summer the whole building is adorned with floral displays of hanging baskets. The bar area is extended through two former rooms. There is a wooden-panelled bar with six beer taps, quarry tiles and wooden floors throughout and real fireplaces. A leaded glass panel featuring the pub's name is at one end of the bar and an assortment of framed awards at the other – testimony to the pub's high standard of catering, quality of ale and recognition as a CAMRA Pub of the Year.

SAMBROOK: *THREE HORSESHOES*

Sambrook, Newport, TF10 8AP – 01952 551133

Take the Sambrook road turn from the A41 Chester Road near Hinstock. The pub is at the edge of the village. There is a local bus service to Newport.

Sambrook is an old agricultural village in an isolated rural district, south of Market Drayton, one of four small townships in the parish of Cheswardine. It is 3 miles to the canalside Wharf Tavern at Goldstone (Chapter 6), and a mile further to the Red Lion brew pub at Cheswardine (Chapter 1); both are easily reached by pleasant, quiet lanes, footpaths and the canal towpath.

The village's name has changed variously. It was originally called Sembra in the Domesday Book and possibly derives from 'Sand Brook' from the sandstone that the Showell Brook flows through. The village was later known as de Sambro then Sambrok before finally adopting its present name. On the outskirts of the village, St Luke's Church and two former mills – with millponds – sit by the course of Showell Brook which makes its way to the River Meese, half a mile south of the village. Also nearby is Sambrook Manor, which dates back to 1702. By 1800, the village had two blacksmith's forges, tailors, shoemaker, bakery and mason. The postman walked 4 miles from Newport to deliver letters, staying in the village to collect letters to take back in the evening. The village eventually got a post office but today it is marked for closure, sadly a trend seen in many Shropshire villages. The pub, however, survives although it closed for three years and only reopened in 2004.

Three Horseshoes, Sambrook.

Landlord Kevin Grimston with Mandy and Mandy, regulars from Hinstock.

The Three Horseshoes undoubtedly gets its name from one of the village blacksmith's forges, which was either on the site of the pub or nearby. There was also once a small slaughterhouse and butcher at the pub. The building still stands beside the entrance to the yard; inside are hooks and a carousel for moving the strung carcasses still in situ. The pub is Victorian and about 150 years old, a true rural village local with cheerful good-natured clientele – although not many come from the village. The pub attracts visitors from the whole district who come to sample the extensive range of real ale from five hand pulls that include regular and guest ales.

There is a cosy public bar with quarry tile floor and a radiant open fire, with comfortable stools, tables and high-backed benches. The adjoining restaurant serves well-priced home-cooked food and there are ever-popular curry evenings. A smaller lounge, furnished with Chesterfield sofas and a real fire, adds to the unhurried and relaxing atmosphere.

At one time village 'wakes' were held on the village green, a tradition which originated from the annual commemoration of church dedications. From the Industrial Revolution the tradition was adapted into a regular summer break, a 'Wakes Week', the forerunner of the summer holiday. Landlord Kevin Grimston and wife, helped by a dedicated team of organisers and helpers, have revived this tradition, with a real purpose, fundraising for Severn Hospice and the Juvenile Diabetes Research Foundation. Each summer the Three Horseshoes hosts a charity festival. In 2008 a dozen bands including Airbag, Driftwood, The Epic and Blade performed over the three-day event, with a car boot sale, promise auction, hog roast, ice cream van and a bouncy castle adding to the attractions.

SELATTYN: *THE CROSS KEYS*

Glyn Road, Selattyn, SY10 7DH – 01691 650247
www.thecrosskeys-selattyn.co.uk

Follow B4579 Oswestry to Glyn Ceiriog road, 3 miles from Oswestry

Listed in CAMRA's National Inventory of Heritage Pubs and one of the oldest buildings in the village, the Cross Keys is the perfect embodiment of an English village pub. Stone-built with a whitewashed exterior, the pub has four small bar rooms, each with period charm. The Victorian counter in the public bar is the servery to the corridor that connects the other rooms.

A self-catering holiday flat joins on to the pub. It was previously the village shop and granary which closed in 1994.

The pub has been licensed as an inn since 1880. Former landlords during the last century were Joseph Davies who held the licence from 1900 to about 1920 and Oliver Parry between 1920 and 1939. Bill Jones bought the pub from Banks's brewery in 1939 and was landlord until 1989. The present licensee is Philip Rothera and wife, Hilda, who bought the pub in 1989 after seeing it advertised in a newspaper.

The pub relies on the whole district for its trade as the population of the village is insufficient to sustain a regular clientele, although there are a few regular die-hard customers. Instead, the pub relies on its enviable reputation as an unspoilt Shropshire village pub – with an excellent choice of beer – to attract customers from further afield, especially on Thursday evenings for live Irish music. The Cross Keys does attract local customers on the special occasions when villagers meet and celebrate Christmas, New Year or some other event. The owner is willing to open earlier to accommodate prearranged pilgrimages from CAMRA or other groups.

The Cross Keys, Selattyn.

The picturesque lane leading to the Nant Valley.

The Cross Keys, symbol of St Peter, and hoist to the former granary.

The name of the pub probably has a religious connotation; crossed keys are the symbol of St Peter or the pope. The church opposite the pub, however, is dedicated to the Virgin Mary. St Mary's has an impressive fourteenth-century carved barrel roof over the chancel. Parts of the walls and a blocked doorway are Norman; the font is thirteenth-century and the tower dates back to 1704. The lane that runs between the pub and the church lych-gate drops down into a steep-sided valley called the Nant, the western slopes formed by Selattyn Hill on which stand a Bronze Age burial cairn and a commemorative tower to Gwyn, a sixth-century British prince slain in a battle against the Prince of Powys. Offa's Dyke passes a mile to the west of the village. Offa, King of Mercia (757–96), had this earthwork built as a defence against attacks or raids from Powys. The views from Selattyn Hill encompass the expanse of the Shropshire Plain, the Berwyn Mountains, the Wrekin, Church Stretton, the Breidden Hills and Long Mountain at Welshpool. To the south-east of Selattyn village is another monument: Castle Brogyntyn, a ringwork castle in the parkland of Brogyntyn Hall. The lanes, paths, heath, woodland, valleys, streams and hillside where the Shropshire Plain meets Wales makes a most attractive setting for this seventeenth-century pub. Assured of a friendly welcome, it is a perfect place to complete a walk or to spend an evening by a warm open fire.

Landlord and local bell-ringer Philip J. Rothera (centre) entertains members of the Hereford and Worcester branch of CAMRA, who by chance also happen to be bell-ringers.

Mark Haslam from the Hereford and Worcester branch of CAMRA raises a glass to the Cross Keys.

STIPERSTONES VILLAGE: *STIPERSTONES INN*

Stipperstones, Snailbeach, SY5 0LZ – 01743 791327
www.stiperstonesinn.co.uk

Use local roads from A488 through Pennerley from the south or Snailbeach from the north. There are bus routes from Shrewsbury and Bishop's Castle and the Shropshire Hills Shuttle runs between May and September.

A pub since 1850, the Stiperstones Inn is named after the spectacular 6-mile ridge which rises above it. Sheltered on the western slopes by Oak Hill and Green Hill, the inn blends into an area of outstanding geology, surrounded by ancient castle mounds and remnants of nineteenth-century lead mines. Nestled into a dingle with a small stream running beside it, the inn stands on the lane which joins the two hamlets of Tankerville and Pennerley with Snailbeach lead mines. Ideally placed for walking and touring, there is no better starting point to walk up to Scattered Rock and the Devil's Chair, over purple moorland, to the summit of Stiperstones. For over a quarter of a century the inn has also been the starting point for an annual Boxing Day race run up the Stiperstones. Established by Landlord John Sproson and brother Geoffrey it is now a serious competitive race and attracts athletes and hundreds of visitors to the pub.

The Stiperstones Inn, Stiperstones, a watercolour by Ken Bromley. (*Courtesy Stiperstones Inn*)

A haven for walkers.

The lounge bar.

A traditional family-run free house, the Stiperstones Inn offers guests morning and afternoon teas, real ale and cider from the barrel (aptly named 'fall down in ditch'). There are function and conference facilities, a beer garden and a separate dining room with an extensive menu served daily. Former landlord John Sproson's niece, Lara, runs the pub with Phil Jones. John now spends his time running the adjoining village shop, truly open all hours: 8 a.m. to 8 p.m. every day although he shuts early on Christmas day. To use his words, 'I open on Christmas in case some one forgets to buy sprouts for Christmas dinner.' Another one of John's interests can be found at the back of the pub car park; a paddock and stable are home for two retired racehorses Bevier (15) by Nashwan and Soothfast (19) by Riverman – both race winners.

In the front bar room is a brick fireplace with real fire, conventional stools and tables, old-style jukebox and dartboard. The front lounge next to it has wood panels, wooden beams with an assortment of brassware and local artwork on display, a favourite spot for walkers to enjoy a plate of curly fries with their pints. Two separate restaurant areas are at the rear of the pub. The upper storey room has a huge mirror on one wall and a deer head trophy on the adjacent wall. Not surprisingly, with all its additional services the Stiperstones Inn is a pub that continues to receive much recognition and praise for its role as the hub of the community.

The Very Desirable Fully-Licensed Property

KNOWN AS

THE STIPERSTONES INN

AND

27 Acres of Excellent Dairy Land

The Inn occupies an extremely good position for business purposes on the main road, and has the following accommodation:—Parlour, Bar, Large Kitchen with range, Back Kitchen with grate, oven and two boilers, Large Club Room, Dairy, Pantry, Cellar, Six Bed Rooms.

The Farm Buildings

are built of stone, timber and slate, and include Stabling for Six Horses, with Granary over, Cowhouse with eleven ties, Calf's Kit, Cart Shed, Two Pigstyes.

The Land all lies very conveniently, and is intrinsically rich, and by itself forms a Holding which would pay well; in conjunction with the Inn, a really good business could be done by an energetic owner.

SCHEDULE.

ORD. NO.							ACREAGE.
694	...	...	...	...	...	...	·644
695	...	...	...	...	...	...	4·942
712	...	...	...	...	...	...	2·238
713	...	...	...	...	...	...	3·055
713A	...	...	...	...	...	...	·534
714	...	...	...	...	...	...	·710
715	...	...	...	...	...	...	6·055
716	...	...	...	...	...	...	2·431
793	...	...	...	...	...	...	3·913
794	...	...	...	...	...	...	·828
794A	...	...	...	...	...	...	·345
795	...	...	...	...	...	...	·218
796	...	...	...	...	...	...	·236
797	...	...	...	...	...	...	1·200

27·349

This Lot is let, together with Lot 20, on a Yearly (Lady-day) Tenancy to Mr. T. Stephens at a Rent of £51 2s. per annum, the Rent of this Lot shall be apportioned at **£48 per annum.**

The Commuted Tithe Rent-charge is £2 9s. 6d.

12

Portions of the Minsterley estate for sale by auction at the village hall, Minsterley, on Thursday 16 March 1922.

In the pub's shop – John behind the counter with Roy, a local potter from Tankerville Pottery and Gallery.

Retired racehorses Bevier and Soothfast look on from the paddock behind the pub.

STOTTESDON: *THE FIGHTING COCKS*

High Street, Stottesdon, DY14 8TZ – 01746 718270

At the centre of the village of Stottesdon, reached by country lanes east of the B4363 and west of the B436. Bus stop is outside the pub for Ludlow and Bridgnorth. The Countryside Explorer shuttle runs from April to October between Bridgnorth, Stottesdon and Highley

L oss of amenities, infrastructure, services and places for people to meet has become something of an inexorable process in Shropshire's rural communities. In 1938, the isolated village of Stottesdon lost its railway passenger service. Trains once called at a small halt on the Cleobury Mortimer and Ditton Priors Light Railway, known locally as the 'Ratchet'. The closure was inevitable since the station was over a mile away from the village it purported to serve and passenger train services were sparse: Monday, Wednesday, Friday and Saturday, with never more than one or two trains in each direction a day. Local

farmers started to use road transport to get their produce to market while the villagers got a bus service. The railway continued to carry minerals from local quarries up to 1957 and later the admiralty used it to transport armaments to a depot at Ditton Priors – the line finally closed in 1965. In recent years the village lost a petrol station, convenience store, post office, a pub and brewery, but vehemently holds on to its primary school and church.

The Fighting Cocks, Stottesdon.

In the village shop, landlady
Sandra Jefferies serves a
villager.

In the bar.

The Fighting Cocks is therefore a remarkable survivor, a country pub that remains
open against a background of rural decline while other similar pubs in villages
throughout Shropshire have closed. Stottesdon's other pub was the Fox and Hounds, an
old-fashioned home-brew pub with a skittle alley. It regularly appeared in the CAMRA
guide and its closure in 2001 was a poignant reminder to beer-drinkers and villagers
alike of just how venerable the village local has become. Originally a coaching inn at
the centre of the village and first registered as a public house in 1830, the Fighting
Cocks is the quintessential village pub, half-timbered with plenty of exposed beams
and old world charm. Friendly, warm and inviting, it offers a wealth of services to the
community and a hearty welcome to the visitor from further afield.

The two-level front bar is decorated with garlands of hops and serves a choice of
real ales and a selection of whisky. There is an intimate upstairs seating area which
also has Wi-Fi. The recently renovated stone outbuilding adjoining the pub serves as a
function room for local societies, family reunions, church gatherings, business meetings
and farmers' veterinary seminars. An open fireplace and oak mantlepiece (reclaimed
from a local farm) and exposed wooden roof beams add to the overall charm. The room
serves as a retreat for the more sedate clientele on Monday evenings when the pub
really comes alive with 'Open Mic' sessions, hosted by charismatic singer-songwriter
Jake Flowers – always popular and well supported.

Owner Sandra Jefferies would often be asked by diners in the pub's restaurant where she got her local meat and seasonal produce. To further the wishes of the customers she began to sell vegetables, cheese and bread in the walkway beside the pub. Eventually, with perseverance and support from the Countryside Agency and The Pub is the Hub network, a full-time shop was opened adjoining the pub. The shop sells a wealth of free-trade local produce and groceries, including ethical cleaners, fresh bread, dairy products, locally-produced meat (also home-reared pigs), smoked products, cakes and chocolates. It is a showcase of the very best food from Shropshire and Worcestershire. The Fighting Cocks is a perfect example of a historic Shropshire pub and much more, since it also shows how a pub can benefit an isolated community and how it can be a focus for village life.

Talented singer and songwriter, Jake Flowers hosts and performs on Monday evening Open Mic night.

WROCKWARDINE: *THE BULL'S HEAD*

Plough Road, Wrockwardine Wood, TF2 7AW – 01952 613181

Take the Wrockwardine Wood Way (B4373) from Queensway (A442) and head west to New Road. Turn into Plough Road and the pub is opposite Parkinson's butchers shop. The car park is behind the pub. Bus service from Wellington and nearest railway station is at Oakengates, over a mile away.

In 1898 the parish of Wrockwardine Wood was absorbed into the new urban district of Oakengates, and then in 1968 it became a designated area of Telford new town. Like much of the surrounding district, Wrockwardine Wood was heavily industrialised and intensively mined for coal from the seventeenth century onwards. The Bull's Head stands practically in the centre of Wrockwardine Wood, an area bound by Donnington Wood to the east and Wombridge to the west. The eighteenth century saw the area criss-crossed with canals and the nineteenth century brought railways into the locality. The canals disappeared long ago and the extensive system of railways closed in 1959, but not before it expanded to 26 miles of track, which carried over 1.5 million tons of minerals, coal and goods.

The inhabitants of Wrockwardine Wood worked in the local coal, iron, and steel works. With these industries in decline in the later part of the twentieth century, the sprawling industrial landscape which Wrockwardine Wood had become, gave way to new private and council housing estates. Not surprisingly, the social life of this large working population centred on pubs and by the late nineteenth century there were about eight public houses and fourteen beer sellers. The Jones family with Mr James Jones, the

The Bull's Head, Wrockwardine Wood.

Lavishly tiled interior of the front bar.

Friendly banter at the bar.

landlord, a former stone miner, his wife Rebecca and four children ran the Bull's Head from 1871 to 1881. The pubs of Wrockwardine Wood were home to clubs, societies and lodges of various orders, including gentlemen's clubs, miners' groups, sports clubs and football teams. Many of these have survived to this day. The Bull's Head pub is a prime example of a pub that is part of the community and a social focus, although its present owners had to rescue it from nine months' closure before it reopened in March 2005. True to these traditions, the Bull's Head is headquarters to a football team, which plays in the Telford Sunday League with its home pitch at Hadley Learning Centre.

A typical brick-built Victorian terraced pub, the sign over the front window claims that the premises were established in 1838. In the early part of the twentieth century it underwent a spectacular transformation with a face-lift of encaustic tiles, which remain today. The front upper storey of the building is dressed in large green tiles while the lower storey has a large engraved double window flanked by brown tiled columns and inlaid with a patterned mosaic. The pub has expanded into the adjoining terraced house and has a bar extension at the rear, with pool table and TV for showing sports events. The front bar – identified as the Spirit Vaults from the engraved windows – is lavishly decorated with encaustic tiles laid out in geometric patters. The floor is covered with plain glazed tiles and in the corner of the room is a wood burner. The hardwood bar counter has inlaid panels and a carved wooden back inlaid with mirrors and shelves.

THREE

Shrewsbury Pubs

The historic and economic events that shaped Shrewsbury also had a profound influence on the way the town's pubs developed. Shrewsbury stands on a promontory wrapped by a large bow in the meandering River Severn, a natural choice of location for defence against attack and a ready-made route for trade. The earliest mention of the town is in 901 when it is referred to as Scobbesbyrig, meaning fortified place in the scrub, a reference to the fortification of the town by Ethelfleda, Lady of the Mercians and daughter of Alfred the Great, defender against the Danes to the east and the Welsh to the west. The Norman invasion and defeat of Harold's army at Hastings resulted in significant political change in Shropshire as a whole, and Shrewsbury in particular. William the Conqueror granted power and lands (the Marches) to his supporters and kinsmen for service to the Crown. Roger de Montgomery received the earldom of Shrewsbury and the right to erect castles, a symbol of the authority of a Marcher Lord. During the troubled years that followed, the town became a stronghold and a fortress against the Welsh. The Market Hall at the centre of the town, built in 1596, heralded a more prosperous time for the town when alehouses, inns, taverns and riverside pubs sprang up to take advantage of a flourishing wool trade. By the time Henry Tudor took the throne there were many more inns and taverns in the town – increasing in number during the reign of the Stuarts – regulated by local justices and town authorities.

The Industrial Revolution brought about a similar revolution in transport; canals started to transport coal and goods and improved roads brought more travellers through the town. Taking advantage of this increase in commerce, the first canalside inns opened and coaching inns came to prominence. Public houses appeared in large numbers during the early years of the nineteenth century as a result of the Beer House Act of 1830. The arrival of the railways, heavy industries and the doubling of the town's population also influenced the increase in the number of market taverns, back street locals and the railway inn. Brewing had also become one of Shrewsbury's major industries with the Maltings at Ditherington and the Circus Brewery at Bridge Street supplying an ever-increasing demand. Today the town's brewing industry is gone and pubs are in decline but a few examples of Shrewsbury's old historic pubs survive.

The Hole in the Wall, Shrewsbury, in its civic setting.

SHREWSBURY: *COACH AND HORSES*

Swan Hill, Shrewsbury, SY1 1NP – 01743 365661
www.odleyinns.co.uk

Use town centre parking. Swan Hill is just off Market Street and the Square, a third of a mile from railway and half a mile to bus station.

The Coach and Horses is a nineteenth-century pub at the corner of Swan Hill and Cross Hill. It has been a licensed premises since 1831 and, for its entire existence, a typical town local. It has been extended and refurbished into adjoining buildings to make provision for additional dining areas. Overall, the alterations have not dramatically changed the pub's exterior appearance and the pub is immediately recognisable as a Victorian public house by the white-painted round frontage and corner entrance. Inside the main public bar there is a large bar counter and a screened-off snug; the plaster work has been stripped off to reveal exposed brickwork and the floors are authentic quarry tiles. The remaining bar rooms were altered by the makeover and extension.

The adjoining buildings – part of the extension to the pub – look like separate terraced houses, blending well with the pub to give the traditional feel of a town street. A blaze of hanging baskets on display each spring and summer make all the buildings look attractive and inviting. The Coach and Horses is a true local with friendly bar staff on first-name terms with the predominantly local clientele. The bars serve a wide selection of Shropshire ales, guest beers and excellent food in a pleasant, relaxed atmosphere with live music on Sundays in the lounge restaurant.

The Coach and Horses, Shrewsbury.

A friendly welcome at the front bar counter.

The view from Cross Hill with floral display.

In the early part of the twentieth century a number of the pub's clientele would have been off-duty police officers as the Shropshire Constabulary Borough Police Station was next door to the pub. The address of the police station is immortalised in the song '23a Swan Hill' by Ian Hunter (born Ian Patterson) of the 1970s pop group Mott the Hoople who spent his teenage years there when his father was the station sergeant. In 1900, the owners of the Coach and Horses were Worthington & Co. of Burton upon Trent and in the early 1930s, after the breweries merged, Bass Worthington. The pub is now part of a small group of pubs, Odley Inns Limited (also the Bell and Talbot, Bridgnorth, chapter 2), and features regularly in the CAMRA *Good Beer Guide* along with its neighbour a little further down Swan Hill, the Admiral Benbow.

SHREWSBURY: *THE DUN COW*

Abbey Foregate, Shrewsbury, SY2 6AL – 01743 356408
www.theduncow.co.uk

Off Abbey Foregate, the pub has its own car park.

The first Earl of Shrewsbury, Roger De Montgomery, raised the Benedictine Abbey at Shrewsbury dedicated to St Peter and St Paul, built on the site of an earlier Saxon church east of the English Bridge and the River Severn. Two monks from Sées in Normandy directed the building and, together with a group of master stonemasons, lodged in a building which later become the Dun Cow inn. After the abbey was completed and monastic life was established, the lodgings served as a hostelry for pilgrims visiting the shrine of St Winifred. A large part of the abbey fell derelict after the Dissolution of the Monasteries but the church and refectory pulpit survives. The abbey hostelry then lost its ecclesiastical purpose and became an inn. It was converted and extended in the 1590s using ships' timbers from captured Spanish Armada vessels broken up and transported up the River Severn from Bristol.

The curious name for the Dun Cow is associated with a local fable dating back to the tenth century, a moral tale of plentiful bounty lost through malevolence and greed. One version of the story tells of a cow kept at Mitchell's Fold, a Shropshire Neolithic stone circle. The cow belonged to a giant, and gave a boundless supply of milk until an evil witch milked it dry through a sieve. Enraged, the beast broke loose and escaped creating carnage where ever it went. Eventually the cow found its way to Dunsmore Heath in

The Dun Cow, Shrewsbury.

Warwickshire, where it was slain by Guy of Warwick, putting an end to the terrible rampage. The witch was turned into a pillar of stone for her wicked act, one of many that stand at Mitchell's Fold. The Dun Cow is particularly well haunted and the pub's most famous resident spectre is a Dutch Cavalry officer who, after an altercation that resulted in the death of a town steward, was arrested, trialled, found guilty of murder, and summarily hanged on a hastily erected gallows in the stable yard behind the inn. The Dutchman is reported to have vehemently protested about the injustice saying, 'But I only killed one Englishman!' The protests, jangling of spurs, stomping and occasional manifestation have been heard and witnessed at the Dun Cow on many occasions since.

Nineteenth-century improvements on the London to Holyhead turnpike brought a new prosperity to the Dun Cow. The inn was well placed to serve the passing trade offering accommodation, stabling, food and a brewhouse for beer. After the coaching era, the inn witnessed the coming of the railways. Important main lines from Birmingham and Hereford converged at Holy Cross behind the Abbey Church, although the line that terminated at Abbey station behind the Dun Cow was far from important and struggled to survive for most of its existence. The Shropshire & Montgomeryshire Light Railway operated a sparse rural service to Llanymynech. All the stations closed in 1933, but the platform and derelict station building at the abbey survives and may one day be restored.

Two carvings in the old timbers, a pig . . .   . . . and a sea captain.

The grandfather clock and inviting fireplace in the main bar.

Behind the inn there is a large customers' car park, a former brewhouse and stables next to a smart open-air wooden-decked dining area. At the front of the building is an ancient oak door, held on heavy iron hinges, and a statue of the Dun Cow sits over the porch. In the bar there is a large counter and wooden beams, one beam with a carved figure of a sea captain and another with a pig's head. A small part of the wall is exposed to show the wattle and daub construction underneath and some walls are wood-panelled. A grandfather clock stands beside an open fireplace with a heavy oak beam mantlepiece. There is a well-appointed restaurant leading off from the bar area with plenty of wooden beams, wine storage racks built into the brickwork and a bread-baking oven as a decorative feature. The Dun Cow has live music and a good selection of real ale. It serves good food and retains many original features.

SHREWSBURY: *THE HOLE IN THE WALL*

Shoplatch, Shrewsbury, SY1 1HF – 01743 264971

Opposite Shrewsbury Retail Market. Use town centre parking. A third of a mile from railway and bus station.

The front of the Hole in the Wall pub is in Shoplatch, between two narrow passages (known as Shuts): Gullet Passage, formerly Gullet Shut and Drayton's Passage, formerly Eddowes's Shut. The two passages lead to the ancient town square and to Market Street respectively. The pub today is a combination of two former inns: the Market Vaults and the Old Hole in the Wall, knocked into one by Mitchell & Butlers brewery in 1985. Much of the interior character of both buildings was lost in the revamp, although the exterior appearance is largely unaltered. The front of the inn opposite Shoplatch has the date 1863 embossed in the lower part of the upper-storey window, under the main entrance to the present Hole in the Wall. When separate, this pub was called the Market Vaults and served Shrewsbury's Corn Exchange and Market across the road. It was also referred to as 'The Market' or alternatively by its unsavoury nick name the 'Blood Tub', the origins of which are uncertain and open to speculation. The neo-Gothic market building opened in 1869 to replace produce and open markets in the town. The old Victorian market building was itself replaced in the 1960s, demolished to make way for a new Market Hall. The Market Vaults stood on the site of the earlier Gullet Inn, recorded in 1527, sold in 1788 and closed by 1793.

The Hole in the Wall, view from Shoplatch, Shrewsbury.

The cellar bar.

The pub from Gullet Passage (formerly Gullet Shut).

The other pub, the Old Hole in the Wall (from which the new combined pub takes its name), stands in Drayton's Passage, the shut from Shoplatch to the Market Street. The name for this pub comes from its location. Literally an opening in a wall confined in the space of the passageway, 'Hole in the Wall' was the local nickname for the inn. The earliest records of this inn date to 1883 when it was referred to as Star Vaults and later as Hughes's Wine and Spirits Vault. Built on the site of a former thirteenth-century stone-built mansion house, in the seventeenth century the cellar remained as part of a debtors' prison. Building and restoration work on the pub exposed parts of the mansion house. With the excavation there were finds of brickwork foundations, pottery and a letter dated 1660 which refers to the Black Death. The interior of the combined pub retains some older features and in a cellar dining area, the ghost of Lady Sarah – who in the dead of night walks through the bar – does not seem to mind the recent changes.

SHREWSBURY: *THE LOGGERHEADS*

1 Church Street, Shrewsbury, SY1 1UG – 01743 344226

The pub is near St Alkmund's Church in the centre of town. Use town centre car parks. The railway station and bus station are a fifteen-minute walk.

The Loggerheads is a traditional back street local with two small front bar rooms, a smoke room and parlour, connected by a red floor-tiled corridor which leads out through the single entrance into Church Street. The church is St Alkmund's, founded in Saxon times and famed for its pre-Raphaelite chancel window. The smoke room of the Loggerheads has wooden floors, painted wooden-clad walls, high-backed chairs, wooden tables and a simple fireplace. A sign painted on the doorway proclaims that the smoke room is for 'GENTS ONLY – until 1975'. Signs similar to this – sometimes just written as the letters 'GO' – once adorned many pub rooms up to the last century, a remnant of a time when women were denied access or actively discouraged from entering many places deemed to be the exclusive domain of men. Typically, this room has no serving counter. Drinks are bought at the servery hatch in the corridor or, at one time, were brought in by the landlord or his wife after the service bell was pressed.

The Loggerheads, Shrewsbury.

Landlord John Badger meeting and greeting.

The alternative Loggerheads sign – a large sea turtle.

The parlour bar has a wood-panelled serving counter fitted with two banks of beer hand pulls. There are wooden floors and panelled wooden walls and the tables are far enough away to allow adequate space for customers standing at the counter. On one of the walls is a painting of a sea turtle, a Loggerhead, which represents the pub's name. A totally different interpretation of the pub's name is symbolised by the exterior sign hanging over the entrance which shows three leopards' heads, after 'Lubberhead', an old English name for leopard – loggerhead a possible corruption of the pub's original name. The pub's former name was the Shrewsbury Arms which suggests that the three leopards' heads might in fact represent the arms of the former Borough of Shrewsbury, first recorded in 1623. Based on a thirteenth-century seal and the colours of Roger de Montgomery, Earl of Shrewsbury, the motto of the former Borough Council also used by today's Shrewsbury Atcham Borough reads 'Floreat Salopia' or 'may Shrewsbury prosper'. The words might well be an echo of a toast drunk in this traditional old public house. The snug at the far end of the entrance corridor is small, cosy and intimate. A well-used fire grate is set into one corner of the room, surrounded by wall-to-wall seating. Off another corridor – in a modern extension to the pub – is the lounge bar, spacious and comfortable, served by another service hatch from the front bar.

Smoke room for gentlemen only . . .

. . . until 1975.

SHREWSBURY: *THE NAG'S HEAD*

22 Wyle Cop, Shrewsbury, SY1 1XB – 01743 362455

Use Wyle Cop or St Julian Friars pay and display car parks. Railway station and bus station half a mile.

Recently restored, this fine old pub is halfway up the steep Wyle Cop, 'ridge top' translated from Welsh, once part of the busy London to Holyhead coach road through Shrewsbury. Wyle Cop has many old buildings, some dating back to early Tudor times. Henry, Earl of Richmond, stayed in one – a half-timbered house opposite the Nag's Head – after the town surrendered to his army on 15 August 1485, the day before he departed for Bosworth Field to defeat King Richard III and take the crown as King Henry VII. The Lion Hotel, another splendid old building at the top of Wyle Cop, is one of Shrewsbury's finest hotels and was originally the town's principal coaching stop for the London and Irish mail. It is steeped in history, folklore and tales of the supernatural.

The Nag's Head, on the steeply sloping Wyle Cop, Shrewsbury.

Looking up to the top of Wyle Cop the
former coach road and the Lion Hotel.

A welcoming smile at the bar.

Like its famous neighbour, the Lion, the Nag's Head is also reputed to be haunted. The
third-floor room of the inn, which overhangs the street, has witnessed three suicides:
a coachman who hanged himself, a young woman, and a soldier heading home from
service in the First World War. These unnatural deaths are attributed to the influence of
a mysterious oil painting on the inside of a cupboard door in the room, a depiction of
a mythical character, Neptune, with a trident. The Nag's Head was also the location for
another ghostly tale in 1984, this time fictional. The unusual timber-framed structure
behind the pub is all that remains of Nag's Head Hall which was used as a set for a film
adaptation of Charles Dickens' *A Christmas Carol*. The Ghost of Christmas Yet to Come
(played by Michael Carter) met Ebenezer Scrooge (George C. Scott) here. The film
production featured other scenes from around Shrewsbury, including Fish Street and the
Three Fishes Inn (see chapter 3). The other apparitions were Marley's ghost (Frank Finlay)
and Edward Woodward, the Ghost of Christmas Present.

The strange painting in the cupboard claimed to exert a supernatural influence on visitors to the room.

The Nag's Head's spacious beer garden – a pleasant spot of green hidden away from the roadside.

The beer garden at the rear of the pub was once occupied by houses and shops, part of a shut and courtyard called Nag's Head Court. The pub first appears in historical records in 1780 but, like the adjoining Nag's Head Hall, dates back to a much earlier period. Part of the equally early medieval fortifications of the town, the town walls are traceable in the courtyard. A popular drinkers' pub, the Nags Head is one of the town's most interesting and unusual buildings and is a frequent entrant in the CAMRA *Good Beer Guide*.

The remains of Nag's Head Hall at the rear of the pub built in 1422; sadly the greater part of the building was demolished in the 1950s. The arched roof truss and screens passage remain with richly decorated panels and mouldings.

SHREWSBURY: *THREE FISHES*

4 Fish Street, Shrewsbury, SY1 1UR – 01743 344793

The pub is in Fish Street next to the High Street. Use town centre car parks. Railway and bus station 450 yards.

> 'High the Vanes of Shrewsbury gleam
> Islanded in Severn Stream;
> The bridges from steepled crest
> Cross the water east and west.'
>
> A.E. Housman *A Shropshire Lad*, 1896

Practically in the centre of Shrewsbury and in the shadow of three church spires, the Three Fishes stands in a quite side street below the steps to St Alkmund's Church. In AD 901, Ethelfleda (daughter of Alfred the Great) granted Shrewsbury's market charter and started fortifying the town. She also founded St Alkmund's Church some ten years later, close to the market. Fish Street takes its name from the open fish market once held there. Part of the once-busy and bustling market centred on the square and St Alkmund's Place. Other nearby streets, Butcher Row and Milk Street, are similarly connected with the market.

Fish Street – called such from at least 1377 – once had four inns, testimony to the busy market. One inn stood by the Bear Steps next to a medieval hall, appropriately called

The Three Fishes, Shrewsbury.

The Three Fishes from the steps to St Alkmund's church.

Bar staff and customers in jovial mood.

the Bear Inn. The others were the Half Moon and the Plough Inn – only the Three Fishes remains. The medieval church of St Alkmund's also disappeared, hastily demolished in 1794 (apart from the tower), when all of Shrewsbury's churches were considered unsafe after the tower of the nearby old St Chad's Church collapsed and crashed into its nave. The decision to demolish St Alkmund's Church later proved misguided as it took many attempts using gunpowder to shatter the walls. The new church opened in 1795 with its most notable feature being the painted-glass east window by Francis Eginton.

The fishmongers, butchers and general market stayed roughly in the same place from the Middle Ages until the Victorian period. The fish boards which hung on the retaining wall opposite the Three Fishes were relocated in 1869, along with other market stalls to the Corn Exchange and Market at Shoplatch. Deprived of its market, the Three Fishes settled down to a quieter life as a local.

The pub, originally called the Fishes Inn, was renamed the Old Three Fishes then the Sportsman and finally the Three Fishes. The pub's location amid the three parish churches of St Alkmund's, St Mary's and St Julian's suggests that its name might also have a Christian connotation, in that three fishes symbolises the Holy Trinity. The building dates from the Tudor period although much altered over the centuries. By the turn of the twentieth century, the pub – a tied tenancy of Southam's Brewery, based in the town – had four public rooms and three bedrooms for paying guests. Today the separate bar rooms have gone, replaced by a single bar and central counter, although the feel of separate rooms is not totally lost in that distinct areas and a number of nooks and crannies are still present. Inside, original beams protrude from the bright white walls and ceilings, unaffected by cigarette smoke because the inn was the first pub in Shrewsbury to implement a voluntary smoking ban, long before the national ban came into force. Freshly cooked food is served daily (except Sunday evenings) along with excellent beers. The pub won the Shrewsbury & West Shropshire CAMRA Branch Pub of the Year award in 2002.

A picturesque view of the Three Fishes, Fish Street, and St Julian's, another of Shrewsbury's churches, in the distance.

FOUR

Mug Houses & Riverside Pubs

For centuries, there was no alterative to the River Severn for the long-distance transportation of goods and people as the county's roads were largely impassable, and former Roman roads had degraded to cart tracks. Since Roman times, and up to the early years of the Industrial Revolution, the Severn was navigable beyond Shrewsbury as far as Welshpool, although boats had to be man-hauled and dragged over rapids and shallows for part of the way. A variety of vessels sailed the river; the best known were the Severn trows of which there were two types: the 'lower trow' which, as its name suggests, worked the lower reaches of the river into the estuary and along the coast and the 'upper trow', a much smaller vessel, flat-bottomed and of lower tonnage, which was better suited for the shallows and rapids upriver. The upper reaches of the Severn were difficult to navigate at the best of times, especially hazardous when the water levels were low during the summer when rocks and shallows were exposed. Teams of up to twenty men pulled together to rope-haul boats upriver. Known as bowhauliers, these hardy, tough men were hired at riverside mug houses where they sometimes spent days laid up drinking, waiting for trade or for sufficient height of water.

The river trade declined by the early part of the nineteenth century, hastened by competition from more efficient, less costly alternative means of transport: canals, turnpike roads and railways. By 1844 the river level of the Severn was raised by a series of weirs downstream of Stourport in Worcestershire, improving navigation over shallows and rock bars. However, the improvements did not extend as far as Shropshire and river traffic in the county declined rapidly as a result. The disappearance of the trow and bowhauling left the mug houses in Shropshire literally high and dry and many closed. A few survived as hostelries, catering for fishermen, tourists and weekend visitors. Distinct from mug houses, some riverside inns stood at crossing places or near bridges and fords, either on the Severn or on Shropshire's non-navigable rivers.

Set back from, and facing the River Severn in typical mug house fashion, Ye Olde Robin Hood Inn, Ironbridge.

BRIDGNORTH: *THE BLACK BOY INN*

58 Cartway, Bridgnorth, WV16 4BG – 01746 764691

Situated halfway along the steep Cartway and approached from either High Town or Low Town. Use town centre car parks. Local buses from High Town and by rail at Severn Valley Railway station connecting to national railways at Kidderminster.

T he Black Boy was originally an alehouse serving the river trade, one of two survivors from possibly twenty-two similar establishments which once stood in Cartway including inns, boarding houses and brothels. The Black Boy's neighbour further down Cartway is Bassa Villa, a small hotel and restaurant which dates from 1591. It is reputedly haunted by 'The Lady in Black' who weeps for the loss of her two children, William and Charlotte, both of whom drowned when the river flooded the cellar in which the children were inadvertently trapped.

Cartway was the steeply-sloped main thoroughfare from the river wharves to High Town prior to 1786 before the New (toll) Road opened. A plaque in Cartway commemorates the location where a carter once lived and where he stabled his donkeys.

The Black Boy stands among picturesque houses in the street and a plaque on its wall describes the pub's history. While the pub's sign is a politically correct depiction of a chimney sweep holding his brush, the pub's name does not derive from a chimney sweep, but from a monarch. Before the restoration of the monarchy and during a time called the Interregnum when England was governed by Parliament, later under the Lord Protector Cromwell, talk of King Charles II (already crowned king of Scotland) was not permitted and considered a punishable offence

The Black Boy Inn, Bridgnorth.

The warm fireplace in the bar.

by the puritan government. It was only possible to speak the king's name in secret; in public he was referred to as the 'black boy over the sea'. 'Black boy' was the nick name given to him by his mother because of his dark complexion, and over the sea because of his imposed exile after his military defeat and flight from Worcester.

Bridgnorth suffered for its allegiance to the Crown, and large sections of the town were destroyed by fire after bombardment from Parliamentarian artillery. The town's defenders were forced to surrender to the Roundheads leaving the town's defensive walls razed and the Norman castle blown up. It is not surprising that Bridgnorth, fiercely loyal to the cavalier cause, should have named a pub after the monarch.

The Black Boy has two cosy bars, both with real fires, a beer garden and an umbrella-covered seated area for smokers. The public bar is the venue for regular live music, including jazz sessions on the last Saturday of the month and special performances promoted by Friends of Shropshire Jazz. The cellar might have once connected to the cellar of the Saracen Arms (Yeoman Cottage) and there are stories of ghosts. Cartway is a particularly haunted part of town and locals have witnessed strange occurrences. A previous landlord was locked in from outside and had to break through part of the wall to get out. The present landlord in his first few weeks at the pub found a penny in exactly the same position on the floor in the bar every day, nuts were thrown about and light tubes exploded in the cellar. All these events have not escaped the attention of local paranormal investigators who have visited the pub to research the cause.

EDGERLEY: *ROYAL HILL*

Edgerley, SY10 8ES – 01743 741242

2½ miles from A5 using local roads.

The eighteenth-century Royal Hill stands in a riverside meadow overlooking the River Severn, in sight of the Breidden Hills. It probably takes its name from the royal residence of a Celtic king who ruled the area from his Iron Age hill fort. The course of the river up to Pool Quay near Welshpool meanders wildly and it was a difficult stretch to navigate. In the winter the Severn was often swollen by the combined floodwaters from the River Vrynwy, and during summer droughts the water level might be insufficiently high enough for a vessel to negotiate the shallows, during which times river traffic was laid up for days or weeks at a time.

Teams of men were employed to haul river craft upstream such as 60ft long trows rigged with a single mast and sail and up to 40 tons of cargo. These bowhauliers – up to twenty at a time – were hired at mug houses along the river, each man's contract sealed with two mugs of ale, two meals and *2s 6d* per day wages. Ideally situated for a mug house, the Royal Hill once belonged to Samuel Higgins, a river trader who owned and operated a trow used to transport stone, quarried nearby. The pub was also at a ferry crossing. By the beginning of the nineteenth century, the Montgomery Canal arrived at Pool Quay and the river trade dwindled away, although timber was carried on the Severn for many years after. The last shipments were aboard the trow *Mary Ann* in about 1870. Admiral Rodney (1719–92) erected a pillar on Breidden Hill in tribute to Montgomeryshire for the timber it supplied to build ships during the Napoleonic Wars, timber being transported to naval shipyards by way of the Severn.

The Royal Hill, Edgerley.

Although the Royal Hill has other more spacious bar rooms, it still retains its small compact public bar, a reminder of how things were before open-plan central bar counters became the order of the day.

During the ever-increasing periods of flooding, landlord John Bewley has found a way to ferry pub-goers to and from the pub and the lane, using an ex-French Army vehicle as the 'flood bus'. The vehicle has proved useful to his neighbours and local farmers who need to reach households and stranded animals. The fire brigade have also shown an interest should the brigade's fire engines, with lower axle heights, be unable to reach a flooded location. In recent years, the riverside terrace in front of the pub has been an overnight stop for canoeists on the 34-mile Pool Quay to Shrewsbury Upper Severn Canoe Rally, held in May.

The pub retains its character and period charm and is listed in CAMRA's national inventory of heritage pubs. It has a number of separate bars. To the right of the front entrance is the front bar and adjoining lounge, joined by a low passageway beside a central fireplace. Both are warm and inviting during cold winter months and there is a servery to the central bar room. The central bar is small and compact and is the service counter for all the other bar rooms. A wooden outbuilding is used for an additional dining room, games and pool room. There is plenty of outside seating and a covered veranda space to accommodate smokers and summer visitors. Cycle Route 81 passes alongside the pub and the source-to-mouth long-distance footpath, the Severn Way, passes nearby. The pub is a perfect stopping-off place for canoeists, walkers and regular visitors.

IRONBRIDGE: *TONTINE HOTEL*

The Square, Ironbridge, TF8 7AL – 01952 432127
www.tontine-hotel.com

Opposite the Iron Bridge.

The impressive looking Tontine Hotel boasts twelve rooms ranging from family rooms to singles. Room five is supposedly haunted by the restless spirit of a fugitive murderer who was discovered hiding there. Apprehended by the authorities and later trialled, he was found guilty and was hanged for his crime, the murder of a landlady at Kettley. The ghost, known as Fred, manifests his presence by turning lights off and reversing the motion of hands on clocks.

The Tontine serves a traditional English breakfast and snacks and meals throughout the day at the bars or in the separate Mexican-style restaurant. The reception hall is tiled with decorative floor tiles and a painted wood and glass partition separates it from the back bar. A passageway connects to the back bar and restaurant. The entrance to the front bar is through a door in the reception hall, and both front and back bars form a large spacious room with high ceilings. Painted walls and large sash windows make the room light and airy and overall there is a feel of grandeur about the pub.

The Tontine, Ironbridge.

The Tontine overlooking the world-famous Iron Bridge, built in 1777–9 by Abraham Darby III.

Although strictly speaking a hotel, the Tontine is still very much a pub and very much a drinking establishment. It is ideally placed in front of one of the greatest icons of the industrial age, the Iron Bridge, from which the town gets its name. The hotel once served merchants and river traders and was a stopping-off place for travellers through the gorge. The bridge dominates the surrounding area and is a scheduled Ancient Monument, recognised as the forerunner to all modern steel bridges.

The name of the hotel came about from the contract made to build it. A tontine was an investment which combined a group annuity and group life insurance, named after the banker Lorenzo de Tonti. Each investor paid into the tontine and each received dividends from the sum invested. As each investor died, the dividend was divided among the surviving investors. The process continued until there was only one surviving investor who received all the dividends. The capital reverted to the state when he or she died. The tontine funded many public works and capital ventures, though Britain eventually outlawed it since it tempted investors to kill one another to increase their share of the profits. Interestingly, a hotel similarly called the Tontine was built to serve the same river trade and the canal at Stourport-on-Severn in Worcestershire. It, however, was less fortunate and after many years of neglect is closed and boarded up; stark contrast indeed to the success of Ironbridge's Tontine Hotel.

The grand entrance hall and spectacular tiled floor.

IRONBRIDGE: *YE OLDE ROBIN HOOD INN*

33 Waterloo Street, Ironbridge, TF8 7HQ – 01952 433100

Take the B4373 from the end of Ironbridge High Street, alongside the River Severn, past the ruins of Bedlam Furnaces. The pub is on the left just before the road turns onto the suspension bridge across the Severn.

Set back from, and facing the River Severn in typical mug house fashion, the Robin Hood Inn stands on the north bank of the Severn against the heavily wooded hillside of Lloyds Coppice, a sweeping backdrop to the river. The name Robin Hood is associated with many places throughout the country, although it is not clear why this pub should have this name. There is a Shropshire story which has parallels with that of Robin Hood and the Sheriff of Nottingham. Fulk Fitz Warine III of Whittington Castle, deprived of his birthright and baronial seat when King John came to the throne and branded an outlaw, embarked on a campaign of robbing from the rich and giving to the poor. He eventually laid siege to his former castle with a band of outlaws taking it from his rival, Sir Morys. He later received a pardon by King John. Another plausible connection with Robin Hood might be the burial mounds called Robin Hood's Butt on the top of Long Mynd (a butt is a mound of earth behind an archery target).

In front of the pub is the new tubular steel- and cable-stayed Jackfield Bridge with a span of 190ft and 39ft-wide carriageway, officially opened in October 1994. This spectacular bridge replaced the so-called New Free Bridge, a toll-free bridge over the Severn, which

Ye Olde Robin Hood Inn, Ironbridge.

The main bar with shiny wooden floor and welcoming fireplace.

itself was an alternative to the famous Iron Bridge. The earlier reinforced concrete Free Bridge was built in 1909 with funds raised by Mayor Maddox. The bridge was designated a Grade II listed structure in 1985. However, progressive decay of the concrete and rusting of the steel reinforcement eventually made the bridge unsafe and beyond repair and it was demolished.

Madeley Wood underwent a period of intense industrial activity. Based on ironstone, coal and clay, the innovative Madeley Wood Company Ironworks opened its furnaces (also known as Bedlam Furnaces) in 1756–7 beside the Severn. The remains of the furnaces stand alongside the road, a few hundred yards away from the Robin Hood. As heavy industry and the busy river traffic reached its zenith, with a fleet of forty trows based at Madeley Wood, two inns served the working population.

The Robin Hood, and its nearby neighbour the Bird In Hand (worth a visit), would have been constantly busy filling mugs of beer for thirsty bargees, bowhauliers, ferry passengers and ironworkers. A different clientele use the Robin Hood nowadays: construction workers and engineers involved in consolidation work on the embankments of the gorge and regular Friday evening tradesmen. The pub regularly appears in the CAMRA guide and attracts the discerning drinker as well as visitors to the gorge's museums and riverside and natural woodlands. The pub has an outside patio overlooking the bridge and the river. Inside the main bar is a shared bar counter between a smaller adjoining bar room. The bars have wooden floors and wooden ceiling beams. A wall and central fireplace separate the rooms.

A tranquil riverside scene with pub and Jackfield Bridge.

JACKFIELD: *THE BOAT INN*

Ferry Road, Jackfield, TF8 8NQ – 01952 882178

Either park in Ferry Road (although parking is limited) or at the public car parks in Coalport, north side of river and cross on the footbridge. Bus route on Coalport side of river.

For over 400 years, Jackfield on the banks of the River Severn in the Ironbridge Gorge was the focus of intensive industrial activity based on coal and minerals dug out of the ground locally. The district had come to prominence by the middle of the seventeenth century with ironworks, brickworks, clay pipe, pottery and encaustic tile works. Ideally placed with wharves between the Iron Bridge and Coalport Bridge, each industry, from brickworks to tile makers, had a loading place on the river and access to the riverbank, some served by an intricate network of tramways and plateways. From the beginning of the eighteenth century, a string of riverside settlements grew up around the wharves and factories. The rows of cottages at Jackfield are an indication of the appearance of these communities. The others disappeared when the river eroded the embankments and houses slipped into the river.

There were three potteries at Jackfield in the eighteenth century making salt-glazed stoneware, fine white stoneware, Jackfieldware and coarse everyday earthenware. By the 1720s there were several 'potworks' or 'mug houses' near the river making tankards with manganese-streaked glaze. Public houses up and down the Severn used a constant supply of these so-called 'mugs', and were referred to as mug houses themselves.

The Boat Inn, Jackfield, true to its boast, genuinely unspoilt by progress.

The regular and ever-popular
traditional Irish music night – started
over twenty years ago – held each
Thursday from 8 p.m. till midnight
with musicians from far and wide.

An attentive ear and pleasant smile to
accompany the music.

Jackfield China works relocated across the river during the 1790s, to take advantage
of ironmaster William Reynolds' canal and the Hay Inclined Plane, which connected to
the national canal network at Blists Hill. The Werps ferry next to the Boat Inn carried
workers to the Coalport China works from their homes in Jackfield. In 1799, the ferry
sank and twenty-nine people drowned. The Coalport and Jackfield Memorial Footbridge
of 1922, built to commemorate those who died in the First World War, replaced the ferry.
The footbridge was refurbished in 2000 through the combined efforts of the Residents'
Association and the Jackfield Branch of the British Legion, supported by the council,
trusts and Lottery.

The Jackfield Branch of the British Legion hold their annual remembrance services at
the foot of the bridge and meet at the Boat Inn on the first Sunday of each month. During
the summer, groups who portray the Home Front during the Second World War stage a
resistance weekend at the Maws Craft Centre and camp on the gardens of the Boat Inn.
The pub was the HQ of Jackfield & Coalport 'D' Company, part of the Ironbridge Battalion
Home Guard, tasked to defend local factories and munitions stores against invasion.

The Boat Inn.

Flood heights recorded in recent times – a constant reminder of how vulnerable the pub is to the River Severn in flood.

The river ferry influenced the growth of the settlement with the Ferry Boat Inn (as it was then known), a popular stopping-off place for thirsty workers from the China works as well as for bowhauliers and bargees. The location of the inn is perhaps a little too close to the river as the pub frequently finds itself engulfed by water from the Severn when it floods.

From the mid-nineteenth century, Jackfield's industries used local coal and clay for the manufacture of bricks and roof tiles. The church, built at Jackfield in 1863 and designed by Sir Arthur William Blomfield, was built with many differently coloured, locally produced bricks and tiles. The arrival of the Severn Valley Railway prompted the establishment of a tile manufacturing industry. The Craven Dunnill tile factory, designed by Charles Lynamand, and the Maws factory built alongside the railway, utilised extensive sidings for transport of tiles worldwide. The factories closed when the fashion for tiles changed after the First World War. The Maws factory, in sight of the Boat Inn, finally closed in 1969 and most of the factory sites disappeared along with the railway. What remains of the Maws works is now part of a craft centre. The Jackfield Tile Museum occupies Craven Dunnill's old encaustic tile works, part of the Ironbridge World Heritage Site.

The Boat Inn is a popular venue for music, with weekly folk spots and an Irish music session every Thursday evening as well as bands and concerts throughout the year. The interior is in keeping with a mug house, sturdily built with solid walls to resist flood damage. Inviting and intimate, the separate bar rooms have open fires, low ceilings and uneven red-tiled floors throughout. There is a single, well-stocked bar counter and an exceptionally warm welcome from staff and locals.

LLANYBLODWEL: *HORSESHOE INN*

Llanyblodwel, SY10 8NQ – 01691 828969

About 6 miles south-west of Oswestry on the A483, cross bridge over River Tanat at Llanyblodwel. Bus service to Oswestry.

Llanyblodwel is a well-hidden picturesque village at the lower end of the Tanat Valley. The Tanat joins the River Vyrnwy – a tributary of the Severn – 2 miles south of the village and a mile from the Welsh border. Offa's Dyke is a little over a mile to the east and neighbouring townships are Abertanatt, Bryn and Llynclys. Until recent times, the whole area was heavily quarried for limestone, copper and lead.

From the north, St Michael's church overlooks the river and village, built on a much earlier religious site believed to date back 1,700 years. The present church with its unusual octagonal tower is the work of the Revd John Parker who rebuilt the earlier Norman church in 1855. The Grade II listed, half-timbered Horseshoe Inn possibly existed in 1445 as a drovers' inn. Locals say that it was originally a hostelry on an ancient river ford, which entered the river between cottages and the old smithy. The bridge, built in 1760, replaced the crossing and possibly an earlier packhorse bridge. The hostelry became a coaching inn at this time, complete with mounting block for horses.

After 1860, the railways arrived to exploit the lucrative mineral traffic of the area. The Tanat Valley Light Railway had a station 150 yards behind the pub. The platform still exists, though it has been closed since the 1950s, and the rails were lifted in the 1960s. With the dreams of rail preservationists coming true, the recovery of long-closed lines from Gobowen, Oswestry, Llynclys and Llanyblodwel Junction is well underway. It has been suggested that the whole Tanat line to Llangynog might one day reopen with the

Horseshoe Inn, Llanyblodwel.

The Horseshoe's single bar . . .

. . . and a warm secluded corner.

possibility of steam trains calling at Llanyblodwel village halt behind the pub; a prospect appealing to drinkers and rail enthusiasts alike.

The main bar is very cosy with a low ceiling, warmed throughout by an Excelsior iron range, decorated with lots of brass kettles. On shelves around the fireplace and the mantlepiece are tankards, glassware and bottles. In front of the hearth is a 10ft long oak table with a high-backed wooden settle. A wood frame separates the bar from the lounge and part of the wattle and daub partition remains displayed in a glass case. The lounge room has a rustic stonework wall on which hang brass ornaments. The room is furnished with rectangular tables and round-backed chairs, with a fireplace at the far end of the room. To the rear of the bar and lounge is another small wood-panelled room, and there is a third bar room on the opposite side of the main entrance, also panelled, and used as a pool room.

Licensees Jessica and Paul Oakley have run the Horseshoe Inn for the past fourteen years. The inn is freehold and is usually closed in the daytime on weekdays and closed all day on Tuesday and opens in the evening. Friday night is busy and a locals' night. The pub is a true drinkers' haunt with a varying selection of local beers, but no meals served at present. The drinkers are not the only ones to haunt the bar; the pub has a number of ghosts. One is a prankster who locks people in the cellar or upstairs bedroom and moves things about. The owners have heard one laughing out loud and seen an apparition of a little old man sat warming himself at the fireplace. On other occasions a woman appears fleetingly in the bar room.

The Horseshoe is an inviting pub for villagers, walkers, rail enthusiasts, the pheasant shoot, anglers and farmers.

SHREWSBURY: *THE BOAT HOUSE INN*

New Street, Shrewsbury, SY3 8JQ – 01743 231658
www.boathouse-shrewsbury.co.uk

At the top of New Street before Porthill Road A488, on foot from town centre via Porthill
footbridge and Quarry Park.

The Boat House Inn stands on the outer west loop of the River Severn, as the river forms a 180-degree loop which practically encircles the centre of the town. Next to the pub is the Porthill Bridge, a suspension bridge which joins Quarry Park with the district of Porthill. The bridge replaced the ferry in 1922. A plaque commemorates its erection by the Shropshire Horticultural Society, Porthill residents and the engineers David Rowell & Co. Ltd of Westminster. Quarry Park, on the inner bank of the loop in the river, is the famous setting for the annual Shrewsbury Flower Show, the world's longest-running horticultural show.

Like the annual August flower show, the Boat House Inn is especially popular during the summer, with its clientele drinking and eating alfresco on riverside terraces, which overlook this particularly tranquil and picturesque stretch of the river. The river appears very different from the time when it was a busy commercial artery and the riverside area was crammed with trows, wharves and warehouses. River trade practically disappeared in the middle of the nineteenth century with the coming of the railways, at about the time when competitive boating started to become a popular pastime for Victorian and Edwardian gentlemen.

The Boat House Inn as it appeared in a postcard view from the 1920s. (*Princess Series R.M. & S. Ltd*) (Author's Collection)

The pub seen from Porthill Bridge.

The Boat House Inn serves as an ideal grandstand to witness competitive rowing events held at various times of the year. At other times, the frequent practise and training sessions of rowers from nearby Pengwern Boat Club and Shrewsbury School boat house sets the scene. The inn at one time hired out its own rowboats; the actual boathouse still exists at the side of the pub and the rope-hauled ferry that crossed the river was also moored here. In the seventeenth century, the Boat House Inn was very isolated and surrounded by open countryside. Cut off from the town by the river, the inn once housed plague victims from the town.

Inside, the lounge areas are open-plan although each dining area is distinct, with space at the bar to choose from a wide selection of real ales. There are views of the terrace, the footbridge and the river from window seats. The interior has lost many original features in successive makeovers, hiding only too well its history, although the exterior appearance of the building preserves old period charm and is little changed from the earliest paintings, photographs and postcards.

FIVE

Highway & Byway

Prehistoric trackways and ridgeways cross over much of Shropshire's high ground. Some date back to Neolithic times, the Bronze Age and Iron Age. These important prehistoric trade routes were for people that inhabited the district. Ridgeways following high ground avoided the dense forest that once covered the county, like the Portway, which crosses the Long Mynd. It survived as a main thoroughfare into the Middle Ages. The Clun Clee Ridgeway and Kerry Ridgeway survived as drove roads well into the middle of the nineteenth century, and with these routes, there were inns serving ale and offering accommodation to weary travellers.

The word 'inn' has a Saxon origin although the alehouse for lodging and entertainment existed from Roman times. Some hostelries were religious houses while others were secular inns offering a bed, food and ale for the traveller and pilgrim. Some Roman paved military roads were still used by wheeled vehicles up to the Middle Ages, although most roads had turned into muddy tracks by this time. By the mid-sixteenth century, stage waggons appeared, heavy, cumbersome and slow, drawn by teams of six or eight horses, which carried an occasional passenger, while most people travelled on horseback or on foot using the king's highways and inns for overnight stops.

During the late seventeenth century, carriages and stagecoaches, which carried passengers, began to appear, adopting the principle of changing teams of horses at regular intervals. Posting inns hired horses or post-chaise carriages with changes of fresh teams of horses to wealthy travellers. With road transport on the increase, the roads soon became impassable. The upkeep of roads, once the responsibility of lords of the manor, monasteries, religious orders and guilds, transferred to the parishes by statute in an attempt to improve the situation. A new heyday for roads and coaching came in the 1820s and '30s with continued expansion and improvement of the turnpike toll roads. Over a thousand turnpike trusts, responsible for over 25,000 miles of roads, improved journey times and brought about a further increase in coaching inns. Nationally by 1835, the numbers of horses used for posting was in the order of 150,000. All needed stabling and feeding at an inn. Passengers staying the night before a departure, changing coaches at scheduled stops or stopping for refreshment were the inns' other profitable purposes.

The days of the fast coach, stagecoach, Royal Mail coach, stage waggon, fly waggon and post-chaise disappeared along with the turnpike and drove route with the coming of the railways. Many inns survived this downturn in business, converted to hotels, others into country pubs, and flourished with the arrival of the motor coach and motorcar.

Most wayside inns and pubs have changed greatly in appearance. Many have been demolished or rebuilt as large roadside pubs and many have become out-of-town eateries. Smaller wayside inns, roadside village pubs and town centre inns have fared a little better and have retained some of their former appearance. This chapter features a few wayside pubs from across the county. Excluded are two notable and excellent coaching inns: the Feathers in Ludlow and the Lion in Shrewsbury, which are primarily hotels.

ASTON MUNSLOW: *THE SWAN INN*

Aston Munslow, Near Craven Arms, SY7 9ER – 01584 841415

Take the B4368 Much Wenlock–Craven Arms road.

The villages of Aston Munslow and Munslow lie on the west-facing slopes of Wenlock Edge in Corvedale. In 1086 the villages belonged to the 1,000 acres manor held by Roger de Montgomery, Earl of Shrewsbury. Both villages are on the Much Wenlock to Craven Arms road which, up to the nineteenth century, was known as the 'Apostles' Way'. It converted to a turnpike in 1756. The Swan Inn stands alongside the road, opposite Lower House farmhouse, next to the lane which leads back to the village and Aston Hall.

Parts of the inn allegedly date back to the fourteenth century, although the wood box frame construction is largely sixteenth-century. Ideally placed as a coaching inn,

The Swan Inn, Aston Munslow.

A happy face behind the bar.

the Swan was first licensed in 1790 (the same year as the Crown in Munslow) and was most likely a wayside hostelry prior to this date. Licensed again in the eighteenth and early nineteenth centuries, and known for a time as the Hundred House (probably because of the meetings of the Lower Munslow magistrates held here), the Swan has all the features of an early coaching inn – its neighbour in Munslow, the Crown, served as the courthouse of Munslow Hundred.

The Swan is Grade II listed and is an L-shaped timber-framed building, with stone, rubble and brick infill walls and a tiled roof. It has multi-storeys with entrances at different heights and has an attic and basement. On the inside, oak beams claimed to be old ships' timbers (some supposedly over 600 hundred years old) support the ceilings and square-panelled framed partitions divide the public bar, lounge bar and dining room. There are two separate dining areas, two function rooms, pool and games room. The inn also claims to have a connection with Dick Turpin. Reported to have stayed there as a boy while an apprentice butcher, a print of the rogue and highwayman is on display in the entrance hall.

The inn is pleasantly located in a landscape of hills, dales and rivers and is a haven for walkers and cyclists. It has a quiet, enclosed garden and meals are prepared daily – seasonal and local – served throughout the week. The games room is for board games, darts, dominoes, pool and the inn sponsors the local Corvedale Cricket Club.

ASTON-ON-CLUN: *THE KANGAROO INN*

Aston-on-Clun, SY7 8EW – 01586 660263
www.kangarooinn.co.uk

B4368 Clun–Craven Arms Road at the junction with the B4369 Broome Road. Nearest railway station Broome on the Mid-Wales Line, ½ mile walk. Bus routes via Craven Arms from Ludlow, Shrewsbury and Telford.

> In Valleys of springs of rivers,
> By Ony and Teme and Clun,
> The country for easy livers,
> The quietest under the sun,
>
> A.E. Housman, *A Shropshire Lad*, 1896

The strangely named Kangaroo Inn apparently gets its name from a job lot of timber used in its construction, or more likely reconstruction since the inn predates the timber salvaged from sailing steamer *Kangaroo* in 1859. The pub, first licensed in 1831, started out as a coaching inn sometime in the latter part of the eighteenth century, alongside the Clun to Craven Arms turnpike.

The village of Aston-on-Clun is the gateway to the Clun Valley, know for its Arbor tree ceremony, a traditional tree-dressing ceremony carried out since 1660, possibly based on even earlier rituals and rites of fertility to the Celtic Goddess Brigit, whose shrine was a tree. The old Arbor tree stood at the village crossroads. It was cut up after it fell down in a storm in 1995 and replaced by a sapling from the original tree.

The Kangaroo Inn, Aston-on-Clun.

A cosy spot by the fire.

An intimate bar room, separate and
distinct from the remainder of the
pub.

Aston-on-Clun has managed to keep this ancient tradition alive. A trust was set up to
keep the tradition going in 1786 by local Squire John Marston and his wife Mary Carter
to commemorate their wedding day. The tree-dressing holiday was abolished in 1859,
but the tradition continued as a wedding pageant to celebrate the Marston wedding. The
queen's silver jubilee celebrations in 1977 revived the wedding pageant and today it is an
annual event in the village calendar.

The pub stands on the side of the road next to a petrol station (once the blacksmith's
forge) and the Clun Road Round House. This rural scene with the pub at the centre of
the village has hardly changed in a century. Inside is an entrance corridor, once part of
the original bar with literature, information and village newsletters on display, and the
adjoining main room has a bar counter facing a fireplace. Another separate and altogether
more private bar is on the opposite side of the of the entrance corridor. It is heated by an
efficient French wood-fired boiler sat in the fireplace. The room also has a finely detailed
and scaled replica of a 2–6–0 Ivatt Mogul steam locomotive (the type was affectionately
nicknamed 'Mickey Mouse') enclosed in a glass case.

BRIDGNORTH: *THE GOLDEN LION INN*

83 High Street, Bridgnorth, WV16 4DS – 01746 762016
www.goldenlionbridgnorth.co.uk

High Street near Northgate. A limited number of car park spaces are available at the rear of the pub (access is via Church Street and St Leonard's Close), otherwise use High Town car parks. Local bus services from High Street, trains Severn Valley Railway – a twenty-minute walk to station.

The Golden Lion stands nestled in between later Georgian buildings on the High Street near to the Northgate – the only gate remaining of the medieval town walls guarding High Town. The pub dates from the seventeenth century when it started life as a coaching and staging inn. A horse-mounting block at the front of the building is a reminder of that halcyon age. Today buses draw up at the front of the building, a far cry from the age when it was a horse-drawn stagecoach or a post-chaise. The block still gets use either as an impromptu seat or a resting place for shopping bags for bus passengers. Access to the courtyard and car park is by the rear of the building along a passageway, between the traditional snug, the lounge bars and the smokers' shelter.

Quoits, darts and dominoes are played in the public bar, with customers' teams participating in local leagues. The bar is uncarpeted with plenty of exposed oak beams and a large collection of cigarette cards in glass frames showing Charles Dickens characters. Pump clips and beer badges adorn the beams of the pub's three bar rooms, representing all the many different brews served over the years. The rear lounge has a large inglenook fireplace and horse brass-lined oak beams. A collection of photographs – taken in about 1910 when William Henry Ford was landlord (1904–20) – is on display

The Golden Lion and North Gate, Bridgnorth.

Golden Lion regulars from all parts of the county.

throughout the pub; the photographs show scenes from the town, including the nearby bridge gatehouse.

The first known licensee was Mary Hughes and at the time the pub consisted of a number of buildings including cottages, stables and a small brewery. The owner was Lord Acton. The stables held horses for staging coaches as well as for racing. The racecourse was at Tasley, a little over a mile north-west of Bridgnorth town centre and race meetings were held there from 1831 to 1939. The pub displays two old photographs of a race meeting in 1908.

Joseph Knight and Thomas Jones were tenants in the nineteenth century. Charles Austin and his wife Mary took over in 1840 and employed three servants, an indication that the pub was a good source of income. At one time, 'Golden' was dropped from the pub's name for a while, when it was just known as the 'Lion Inn'. Martha Andrews took up the tenancy in 1866 and she reinstated 'Golden' to the pub's name, at the same time Lord Acton sold the pub. By 1912, the William Butler brewery owned the pub. In 1960, M&B took over William Butler. The present landlord and owner, Jeffrey Watkins, turned the Golden Lion back into a free house after he bought it from Bass once they had taken over ownership of M&B. The pub serves good cask-conditioned beer and home-cooked lunchtime meals. The pub also boasts five en suite bedrooms for bed and breakfast accommodation. The Golden Lion Inn regularly holds special events and marks St George's Day as a special day, celebrated at the pub for many years. The Golden Lion regularly appears in the CAMRA *Good Beer Guide* and supports the town's regular beer festival.

CLUN: *THE WHITE HORSE INN*

The Square, Clun, SY7 8JA – 01588 640305
www.whi-clun.co.uk.

In the square at the heart of the town on the A488 Bishop's Castle to Knighton road.
Local bus service to Craven Arms and Bishop's Castle.

In the midst of rural South Shropshire, surrounded by hills of outstanding beauty and tranquillity, is the unspoilt and picturesque town of Clun. At its heart is the White Horse Inn, a former posting and coaching inn that dates back to the eighteenth century, cosily nestled between shops and houses of comparable age in the modest town square. Also in the square is the Town Hall, built in 1780, the open arches of which (now enclosed) cover what was once the butter market and town lock-up. The building also houses a museum exhibiting artefacts found locally, some dating back to Neolithic times. Clun's history is indeed ancient. Iron Age hill forts top many of the surrounding hills. Perhaps the best known is Bury Ditches to the north and Caer Caradoc to the south. Offa's Dyke, the boundary between the English and the Celtic-speaking Cymru, passes to the west of the town.

The Norman Marcher castle at Clun was built in the midst of a Saxon settlement. Its outlying borough formed the pattern of streets seen in Clun today and it was constantly besieged during the centuries-old conflict between the English and the Welsh. A charter granted by King John in 1204 allowed the town to hold two fairs, one at Martinmas and the other during May, the likely predecessor to the Green Man Festival. The border town eventually settled down to a peaceful coexistence with its Welsh neighbours and became a rural backwater. The inhabitants of Clun celebrate their folklore to this day and in the process attract visitors from near and far, to share in their sense of tradition.

The White Horse Inn, Clun.

The White Horse Inn's
well-stocked bar.

The well-appointed
dining room.

Landlord Jack Limond plays his part in keeping the town's traditions as an organiser of the May-time Green Man Festival – a celebration of the victory of spring over winter personified in the battle between the Green Man and the Ice Queen on Clun's ancient bridge. The outcome of the battle is never in doubt, the conflict ends with the victorious procession of the Green Man and his entourage through Bridge Street and the Square to the grounds of Clun Castle where he presides over the May Fair. The occasion is celebrated in the square with Morris dancers performing to locals and visitors, a number of whom are looking on from the entrance of the White Horse Inn. The pub also figures prominently in many other events in the area, especially the October Clun Valley Beer Festival.

The White Horse Inn contains many original features including old panelling in the separate dining room. In the main bar is a large, single L-shaped counter, exceptionally well stocked with an excellent selection of real ales, and there is an inglenook fireplace and real fire for the cold winter months. Leading off to one side is a pool room with a dartboard. The pub also offers accommodation for visitors attracted to this exceptionally beautiful part of Shropshire.

The Shropshire Bedlams Border Morris team's strong and energetic performance outside the White Horse Inn during the Green Man Festival in May.

The turn of the ladies: the graceful Martha Rhoden's Tuppenny Dish.

The Green Man and his May Queen calmly await the Ice Queen and her Frost Maidens for the battle on Clun Bridge. The outcome will decide if summer arrives or winter continues in the Clun Valley.

HOPESGATE, MINSTERLEY: *THE STABLES INN*

Drury Lane, Hopesgate, Minsterley, SY5 0EP – 01743 891344

Approximately 10 miles south-west of Shrewsbury. Take Drury Lane off A488 Shrewsbury–Bishop's Castle road. Bus service to Shrewsbury.

The Stables Inn is a former drovers' inn, high above the fossil-rich shale outcrops of the Hope Valley nature reserve. The inn stands in Drury Lane, the drove route from Wales which weaves its way between Callow and Stapeley Hills, past the ancient stone circle at Mitchell's Fold, through Hope Common and then on to Minsterley and Shrewsbury. Two hedge-lined enclosures face each other on opposite sides of the lane; one bounds the car park and the other the grounds of the inn. The enclosures may have had gates added to secure animals while drovers visited or stayed at the inn.

The Stables Inn has a main public bar with a large open fireplace and single serving counter. In the corner is an alcove, which was once private accommodation with a sitting room and adjoining bathroom. The side room is used for dining and once had a separate door to the outside (now blocked off). The room was set aside for the exclusive use of the drovers while the bar was for guests, who had their own entrance. This comfortable, informal dining room caters for walkers, the estate shoot and regular visitors who travel from Shrewsbury, Telford, Shelve and Bishop's Castle to take weekend lunch with a pint.

The Stables Inn, Hopesgate.

Members of the estate shoot relaxing
by the warm fire before lunch.

Landlady Kate, and Molly, the Stables
Inn's resident wolfhound.

The door to the beer cellar is between both rooms. Tradition has it that a dog guarded the
cellar door to prevent any guest sneaking off with a jug of ale. Happily, this tradition is still
alive today; Molly, the owner's impressive wolfhound, diligently guards the same door.

From the early 1900s, the pub was under the tenancy of Southams & Wem brewery,
but since, has been a free house for over forty years. The present owners, Kate and Chris,
both schoolteachers from Reading, came to the area looking for a place to live. They
ended up buying a pub into the bargain! Kate still works as a primary school teacher and
Chris manages the pub; small rural pubs were often run this way, as homes, with public
rooms for selling beer, with one partner going out to work to supplement the family
income. Food is served from 12 noon until 2 p.m. and 7 p.m. to 9 p.m. at weekends.

Both Kate and Chris have transformed the old premises. They have removed plasterwork
to expose stonework walls and taken out an old back boiler to reveal a large open fireplace
complete with heavy wooden lintel. The exterior of the building, once whitewashed, is
now back to natural stone. There is a rich folklore associated with the district – the pub in
particular – and one unusual funerary custom. If there was a local death, the pub door was
sometimes taken off its hinges to use as a makeshift bier for carrying corpses to funerals,
(local cottages were mostly single room affairs with no need for doors). No doubt the wake
was held in the pub when the door was returned.

LUDLOW: *THE BULL HOTEL*

14 Bull Ring, Ludlow, SY8 1AD – 01584 873611
www.bull-ludlow.co.uk

*Use town centre car parks or street parking, railway station two-thirds of a mile on foot,
bus routes to Leominster and Hereford, Kidderminster, Bridgnorth and Shrewsbury.*

Part of the Bull Hotel dates back to the fifteenth century, added to and extended over the centuries. The frontage is Georgian and the yard is Tudor. No longer a hotel, it is now a busy and popular town pub. Probably one of Ludlow's oldest buildings, a portion of the roof in the main building is mid-fourteenth-century and the covered gallery at the rear of the pub has its origins in the fifteenth century, again added to in subsequent centuries. Early records of a building on this site refer to Peter the Proctor's House (1343), but it is likely a building existed here when St Laurence's Church was built in 1199. The first written reference to the Bull appears in 1580 in the will of a Simon Clare, innkeeper, and then subsequently in the will and testaments of various landlords and thereafter appearing regularly in trade directories for the town.

The Bull was badly damaged in 1693 by a mob protesting about a Presbyterian meeting inside. It again suffered considerable damage in 1794, by a fire which destroyed the front façade. The front of the Bull at one time looked very much like its neighbour across the street, the Feathers, Ludlow's premier hotel built in 1619 with impressive and intact timber frontage. The Bull's three-storey frontage was rebuilt after the fire with smooth,

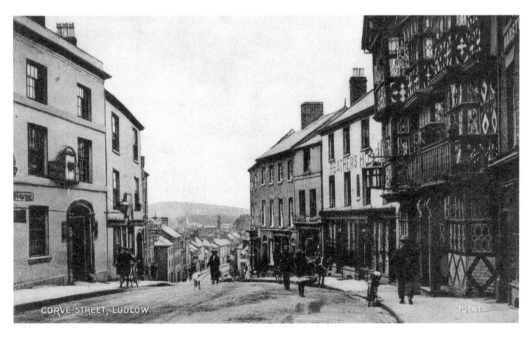

The Bull Hotel on the left, from an early twentieth-century postcard. (*Publisher Unidentified*)
(Author's Collection)

The Bull Hotel's Georgian front façade.

rendered walls. However, from the courtyard of the Bull, entered by the coach entrance, the covered gallery and the rear gable of the main building are as impressive as any of Ludlow's finest half-timbered buildings.

At the height of the coaching era, the Bull's courtyard, bustling with activity, rang out to the stamp of horses' hooves and the trundle of carriage wheels. Overlooked by an open gallery, open to the elements, it was an ideal spot to observe the busy scene. The gallery was also the ideal place to view a performance from a travelling theatre or group of musicians. The gallery, since enclosed and covered, may no longer offer a vantage point for guests to view a performance, but the courtyard still resounds to music during the Ludlow Festival period (between June and July) and at Christmas to New Year – under a marquee-covered stage. At other times the bar is the venue for live music. The courtyard is also an ideal place to eat out on fine days at umbrella-covered wooden tables and chairs.

The coach yard with enclosed gallery.

The lower front bar appears to be Georgian and there are glass cabinets either side of a small open fire grate. A wooden chandelier, in the shape of a wheel with spokes, hangs from the ceiling. The modern bar counter extends through the back bar. Beyond the bar is a comfortable seating area which lies directly below the gallery; the room was at one time an assembly room and a billiards room. The makeover from the 1970s has left a single open space; the intimacy that the separate parlour and smoke rooms once had has been lost, although much of the wooden framework of the interior still exists. Unfortunately, modern fake beams with wooden mouldings detract from any authentic feel. However, there were some discoveries made during rebuilding work: a priest hole and a stepped passageway leading towards the churchyard. Like all inns, the Bull has moved with the times and modernised, perhaps unsympathetically with respect to its interior setting, but it is a friendly and relaxed town centre pub with local food available Monday to Saturday from 12 p.m. to 2 p.m. Consistent with buildings of its age, the Bull has an assortment of ghosts. Footsteps have been heard in the dead of night from the priest's passage, an apparition of a little girl and an old man has been seen, and the mysterious grip of a hand was felt on a former landlord's shoulder when no one was there.

LUDLOW: *THE NELSON INN*

Rock Green, Ludlow, SY8 2DS – 01584 872908

Take the Ludlow road A4117 from the A49 Ludlow bypass, the pub is on the right with car park at rear. Bus routes to Kidderminster and Bridgnorth, and railway station 1 mile towards Ludlow town centre

> 'Authentically grubby'
>
> Dave B (Cheltenham)
>
> 'The finest dysfunctional pub so far'!
>
> Ivor K (Birmingham)
>
> Comments from the pub's visitor book

The Nelson Inn describes itself as a fine example of an eighteenth-century beer house. Throughout Shropshire and the country as a whole, a beer house was a public house in which only beer was sold, although many served spirits under the counter. In 1830, the Beer House Act permitted any household to obtain, on payment of the duties and giving sureties, the right to sell beer and cider. In 1869 the privilege was abolished, but the rights of those in existence were untouched. In this respect the Nelson Inn is true to type. It certainly is a beer house in the sense that the consumption of beer is its main purpose and that its bar and lounge has the feel of being part of an ordinary house.

The Nelson Inn, however, predates the 1830 Beer Act by some fifty years. Originally called the Nelson's Arms, it was built in about 1783 as a coaching inn for two stage routes out of Ludlow. Firstly, the Royal Mail route to Birmingham; the coach departed daily at 3.45 p.m. and ran over the Clee Hills by way of Cleobury Mortimer. Secondly, a Bridgnorth coach skirting the Brown Clee Hills north of Titterstone Clee Hill by way of Burwarton.

The Nelson Inn, a real beerhouse, Rock Green, Ludlow.

Landlord Alan does the honours.

In all probability, the inn may have served as a link stop, where an additional pair of horses was attached to the team to assist heavily laden mail coaches over the Clee Hills. Certainly the Nelson's Arms had extensive stabling with adjoining fields and outbuildings with some half a dozen horses along with a brewhouse.

The name of the pub was changed to the Nelson Inn to commemorate Admiral Lord Viscount Nelson (1758–1805). Many other pubs throughout the country also changed their names in the same way. The uneasy Peace of Amiens was signed between the British and the French in 1801 and Nelson retired to Britain where he stayed with Sir William and Lady Hamilton. The three toured England and Wales, visiting towns and villages. It was on the visit to Ludlow during 1802 when Nelson received the Freedom of the Borough, which prompted the pub to change its name in his honour. The Nelson Inn is a family-run free house, which has appeared in numerous CAMRA *Good Beer Guides* over the years. It hosts two weekend beer festivals, Easter Weekend and one in September to coincide with the annual Ludlow Marches Food and Drink Festival. The pub is a popular venue for live music and hosts regular fund-raising events for the County Air Ambulance and local youth groups. The quality of the beer is exceptional with local and national ales from free trade brewers and there is a Food Special Night each Friday. The exterior white-painted walls of the pub look a little tarnished and there is a clutter of barrels and old inn signs in the yard. Inside is a similar clutter of well-used objects and a well-filled coat rack. The pub looks lived-in and is unpretentious. There is a pool table in the roomy front bar and a comfortable adjoining separate lounge. The smoker is well catered for outside with a suitable wooden structure. The pub has a wide and varied clientele ranging from locals to real ale enthusiasts, all of whom speak highly of jovial landlord Big Alan's genuine beer house.

LYDBURY: *POWIS ARMS*

Church Close, Lydbury North, SY7 8AU – 01588 680254

On the B4385 5 miles north-west of Craven Arms.

The Powis Arms stands at the eastern edge of Lydbury North village beside the north gate of Walcot Hall. The road, today's B4385, is a former coach road which parallels the River Kemp north from its confluence with the Clun, parting with the river as it bears west through the village on its way to Bishop's Castle. To the east is the Jack Mytton Way and to the south-west are the Bury Ditches, an ancient hill fort at the top of Sunnyhill, beyond which is the small town of Clun. Walcot Hall is a large, impressive Georgian house. The former home of Clive of India, it is set in 30 acres of garden and arboretum with a mile-long lake. In the twelfth century, the estate belonged to the Walcot family. It was sold in 1763 to Clive who shortly afterwards commissioned Sir William Chambers to rebuild the house and stable block. When Robert Clive's son inherited the Earldom of Powis by marriage, the family seat moved to Powis Castle. The house and estate at Walcot remained with the family until the 1930s. It was then sold to Ronald and Noel Stevens of Judge Enamel Ware, Brierley Hill, who restored the house and used it – for a time – as a private menagerie and bird sanctuary. Michael Woodbine Parish purchased the house and estate in 1957 as a family home. Walcot now offers holiday accommodation, self-catering apartments, an impressive ballroom for wedding receptions, a riding stables and tours of the house to the public.

The Powis Arms, Lydbury North.

The front bar with a fine selection of whisky.

Inseparably linked with the hall, the Powis Arms adopted its name when Clive of India bought the Walcot Estate. It was formerly called the New Inn. This large building was a coaching inn built at the edge of a sloping hillside on the site of a much earlier hostelry – parts of which exist in the foundations and cellar of the present building. The old road was rerouted behind the inn because it overlooked the hall, so today the back of the inn is actually the front, with the front entrance from the car park. The front bar is at the top of the stairs when entering from the car park and garden, with an adjoining lounge and dining area. A more elaborate dining and assembly room joins this room, lit from numerous iron-framed windows cast at Coalbrookdale. The cellar extends under the entire building, and the servants' quarters were at the top of the building and there were five guest rooms. Today there are four recently refurbished en suite rooms. Evening meals are served in the restaurant which opens between Thursday and Sunday, serving locally sourced traditional English food. The bar and lounge is the village local with a varying selection of real ales and an impressive array of single malt whiskies.

PICKLESCOTT: *THE BOTTLE & GLASS INN*

Picklescott village, SY6 6NR – 01694 751345

Take the A49 north of Church Stretton for 4 miles or south from Shrewsbury for 7 miles, turn west by Leebotwood village, 3 miles on local lanes. The pub and car park is in the centre of the village. Alternatively take road north from Bridges and turn north-west over the Long Mynd. Bus service (May to September) Shropshire Hills Shuttle.

> Into my heart an air that kills,
> From you far country slows,
> What are those blue remembered hills,
> What spires, what forms are these?
>
> A.E. Housman, *A Shropshire Lad*, 1896

Picklescott, or Picklescote, is a small village on the northern slopes of the Long Mynd, within the Shropshire Hills Area of Outstanding Natural Beauty. The village probably existed in late Saxon times, located halfway across a less strenuous route over the Long Mynd range of hills. The Bottle & Glass Inn certainly dates back to the sixteenth century, a former farmhouse before it became an inn, subsequently licensed as a public alehouse in 1837. The village inn prior to this time was the Gate Hangs Well. It still exists as a private cottage and stands on the crossroads in front of the Bottle & Glass. Picklescott Brook flows past the Bottle & Glass Inn and into a culvert under the road. The village was a crossroads over the Long Mynd as it lay equidistant between two former turnpike routes, each from Shrewsbury. The first road headed south to Craven Arms (today's A49), and the second south-west to Bishop's Castle via Bridges. Other roads from the village crossroads joined the Portway east and west of the village.

Nightfall at the Bottle & Glass Inn, Picklescott.

An early evening chat at the
bar.

The wood-panelled lounge
and welcoming hearth.

The inn was a welcome wayside stop when crossing the Long Mynd, especially in winter.
It was used by Welsh cattle drovers, local hill farmers and travellers. The village also had a
blacksmith, wheelwright and carpenter.

Still very much a wayside inn, the Bottle & Glass Inn is popular with villagers, walkers,
cyclists, mountain bikers and horse riders. The bar is extremely cosy, a real drinkers'
spot with a warm fire, red quarry tiles and exposed wooden beams in a low ceiling. The
separate lounge room – with fireplace – is more spacious. An adjoining area at the rear of
the pub, called the library, has a full bookcase and a large table; smaller well-spaced tables
and comfortable seats occupy the lounge surrounded by wood-panelled walls. Next to the
bar is a separate larger dining room with low beams and an open fire for cold days. The
inn has a one-legged ghost, heard on many occasions tapping with his wooden leg as he
walks through the pub, disrupting the electric lighting in the process. The smoking area is
under a large patio heater. The village is picturesque and the hillside offers a spectacular
view of Caer Caradoc, the Shropshire Plain and the Wrekin.

Landlady Paula Gurney and Chilli the bulldog.

WELLINGTON: *THE COCK HOTEL*

148 Holyhead Road, Wellington, Telford, TF1 2DL – 01952 244954
www.cockhotel.co.uk

Take the B5061 Holyhead road, opposite the Old Hall School. There is a pub patrons' car park and a nearby public car park.

A wall plaque at the front of the pub proudly proclaims 'The Cock Hotel, Telford Historic Buildings C18 Coaching House where the Prince and other famous coaches stopped.'

The Cock Hotel stands on Watling Street, an ancient road that dates back to the Roman occupation, an important artery for communication between London and Viroconium (Wroxeter). Constantly in use and after centuries of decay, sections of the road finally underwent a series of improvements by the newly formed turnpike trusts. After 1801, the Union of Ireland and Great Britain meant rule from Westminster, and Irish MPs and the state needed to communicate with Dublin and the Irish principality, important because Ireland comprised a third of the population of the Union. The turnpike trusts struggled to keep this busy route in good repair. The brilliant engineer Thomas Telford eventually carried out huge improvements to the London to Holyhead road over a period of fifteen years. Telford's Holyhead road followed stretches of Watling Street but diverted via Coventry, Birmingham, Shrewsbury, Bangor and across the Menai Strait. Before being diverted, the road passed south of Wellington following today's B5061 (the old A5). Like all great roads of the time it was used by coaches, drawn by teams of horses changed at 10- to 15-mile intervals.

The Cock Hotel, Wellington, Telford.

Table service for CAMRA members Mike White and Dave Hughes in the Old Wrekin Tap.

Wellington was Shropshire's second largest town (before being absorbed into Telford) and between 1830 and the arrival of the railway in 1849 was served by no fewer than a dozen London-bound coaches every day. Many stopped at the two principal posting inns outside the town: the Cock Hotel or Falcon Inn. The Falcon is now a prestigious and fully refurbished hotel renamed the Old Orleton Inn. Coaches with grand names like Wonder, Salopian, Greyhound, Prince of Orange, Prince of Wales, Young Prince, Shamrock Union, Oxonian and the Royal Mail departed from Haygate and the Holyhead road daily. The Cock Hotel staged the Royal Mail coach when it called day and night to pick up and deliver mail and passengers. The mail coach seated four passengers inside and three more outside behind the driver. Inside cost 5d per mile while outside was half the price, and passengers paid the innkeepers along the route. Mail locked in a mailbox was carried in the hind boot, under the post guard's feet, and parcels were kept under the coachman's feet in the foreboot.

For the lager-drinkers, the Brasserie De Haan . . .

. . . with a bay window overlooking the crossroads at the Holyhead road, one time stagecoach route to Anglesey.

When the golden age of coaching ended with the coming of the railways, the Cock Hotel relied on passing trade from the A5 road. Today it survives by virtue of being Wellington's best real ale pub, frequently appearing in the CAMRA *Good Beer Guide* and winner of the local pub of the year award.

The pub has two separate bars. The main bar is called the Wrekin Tap with eight hand-pulls serving a variety of locally brewed ales and regularly changing guest beers – including mild and porter. The large service counter extends across half the room and there are plenty of tables, chairs and padded benches against the walls. The adjoining Brasserie De Haan bar caters for the lager-drinker and has a fine selection of draught and bottled Belgian beer, comfortable seating and a large bay window looking out at the crossroads.

SIX

Canal & Railway Pubs

The Industrial Revolution between 1750 and 1850 spurred a similar revolution in transport. New manufacturing industries required fuel and raw materials, while finished goods needed to be shipped to the ports and burgeoning towns and cities. Since the earliest times, the rivers had been the principal arteries for commerce and trade and during the first part of the eighteenth century, canalisation of natural rivers had extended navigation. However, as the Industrial Revolution unfolded, the need to reach wider markets inland became an urgent requirement. Transport over water was easier; therefore, a system of artificial waterways was a plausible solution to the transport needs of the time.

Most importantly, the need to move minerals and fuel to factories, even over short distances, was proving difficult. The earliest canals were therefore local concerns, promoted by coalmine owners, industrialists and ironmasters who had the funds to build them. Inevitably, as the advantages of canals and their prosperity became apparent, more schemes came before parliament, culminating in the 'canal mania' of 1793 when plans for twenty new cuts were put before parliament, with a share capital of almost £3 million. By 1835, the extensive network of canals that criss-crossed the country and included the Shropshire group, had reached its final complexity. Consequently, just as had happened on the navigable rivers, inns sprang up to serve the thousands of people employed on the canals, the wharves and inclined planes: boaters, wharf-men, labourers, linesmen and boat builders all in need of refreshment and a place to meet, or stable a horse overnight.

The railway age that followed was practically a rerun of the golden age of canals. By the mid-1840s, investors were once again gripped by a promotional boom. This time it was the 'railway mania' when parliamentary powers for over 9,000 miles of railways and £500 million were promoted by British companies. The network of railways – built in just a few years – was substantially more extensive than that of the canals. Railways linked

Shropshire's railways and canals – the preserved Severn Valley Railway . . .

. . . and on the Llangollen Canal.

virtually every city, town and many villages. Cheap railway travel at a minimum speed of 12mph and a minimum price of 1*d* per mile became available to ordinary people on so-called 'parliamentary trains' (conditions imposed by the government legislation), and railway pubs beside every station offered passengers refreshments and overnight accommodation.

Canal Pubs

During the latter half of the eighteenth century, canals in Shropshire had developed into two distinct types: those with locks 7ft wide and tub-boat canals, which accommodated boats 20ft long by 6ft wide. A complex network of tub-boat canals developed in east Shropshire around present-day Telford to serve the iron works and mines – all are now extinct. The Shropshire Canal, which ran from Donnington Wood to Coalport and the Severn Gorge, is perhaps the best known with a preserved length at the Blists Hill Open Air Museum and at Coalport, 207ft below, connected by the Hay Inclined Plane. The next best-known canal is the Shrewsbury Canal, started by Josiah Clowes and completed by Thomas Telford. It ran from Shrewsbury to an inclined plane at Trench. The canal is famous for some impressive engineering relics such as the Longdon iron aqueduct and guillotine locks.

The Shrewsbury Canal, later converted to take conventional narrowboats, made a connection to the Newport Branch Canal (now derelict), which joined the Birmingham & Liverpool Junction Canal (B&LJ), later the Shropshire Union Canal, the principal canal of the Shropshire Union Railway and Canal Company (SUR&CC). Apart from now-defunct tub-boat canals, the remaining canals in the county still exist and are navigable today; the B&LJ skirts the eastern boundary of Shropshire and the Llangollen Canal and the Ellesmere & Chester Canal are to the north-west. All merged to form the SUR&CC on 3 August 1846.

The canalside pub, an ideal spot to service the boat, replenish supplies and stop for an evening drink and meal.

The coming of the railways brought about the decline and eventual demise of the canals and by the middle of the twentieth century, many were disused or abandoned. Surprisingly, a fair number of public houses on these canals survived – despite the loss of trade – and many became country pubs and locals. With the restoration of abandoned navigations and the ever-increasing popularity of pleasure boating, many pubs have once again become true canalside hostelries. Some now offer convenient moorings and provide facilities like water. The pub mooring is popular with modern-day boaters, most of whom plan their cruise to end each evening near a pub, and, as many canals are restored, those pubs that have lost their canals might conceivably become canalside pubs again.

COALPORT: *BREWERY INN*

Coalport High Street, Coalport, TF8 7HZ – 01952 581225

East end of Coalport High Street, the pub's car park is across the road opposite.

In the last decade of the eighteenth century, a small network of tub-boat canals served Coalbrookdale and Coalport. The Shropshire Canal Company's Hay Inclined Plane brought the canal to Coalport and linked the east Shropshire coalfields with the Severn. The outdoor terrace at the rear of the Brewery Inn was the site of a former brewery from which the pub naturally gets its name. It overlooks a dry section of the Coalport Canal and the River Severn beyond it – unfortunately obscured by trees and undergrowth. The Coalport Canal served the Coalport China works, Tar Tunnel bitumen mine (under the Hay Inclined Plane next to the Woodbridge Inn) and transfer wharves on the River Severn, which lay between the pub and Coalport Bridge.

The Brewery Inn, Coalport.

The Brewery Inn's canalside patio
overlooking the overgrown and now
dried-up Coalport Canal.

In the same yard, Maria Gough (1853–1925),
licensee of the Brewery Inn from the age of twenty,
where her daughter ran the pub for seventy years.

At the top of the Hay Inclined Plane, a length of the Shropshire Canal passes a mineshaft and winding engine entrance to the same mine workings served by the Tar Tunnel, 207ft below. The remains of the inclined plane and the working winding house complete with cage and steam engine are exhibits in the Blists Hill Victorian Town open-air museum.

Ironmaster William Reynolds planned Coalport as a new town to serve the canal and riverside wharves. During the 1790s, he built warehouses, workshops, factories and workers' houses and the town was substantially larger then. Coalport was also sufficiently important to have two railway stations. The L&NW station near to the Brewery Inn served the town from 1861 until it closed in 1952 (the line closed in 1960). Railway cottages survive at the end of High Street. On the opposite side of the river, above the Woodbridge Inn, is the other Coalport station. Belonging to the GWR, this station on the former Severn Valley line closed in 1963. The station building survives as a private residence and the owner offers self-catering accommodation in a pair of beautifully furnished Mk I rail carriages.

The Brewery Inn is a two-storey terraced building, extended into a number of joined cottages, with a lengthy single bar, plenty of wooden ceiling beams and bay windows. In the yard at the rear of the building is a ramp, down which barrels of beer once rolled to the canalside for transfer into tub-boats. Malted grain and hops were carried up the steps to the former brewery. The inn probably dates back to the mid-nineteenth century, with parts possibly as old as 1750. During the early years of the river port, the wharves were busy, noisy places, notorious for rowdiness, drinking and prostitution. The landlord of the Brewery Inn tells of a story once told to him of a boat anchored in the centre of the river with victims of the plague on board. Food and water were taken to the victims and when they all finally died, the boat was torched and allowed to burn and sink with the dead bodies on board. There are also stories of sunken trows and finds in the river, iron ore ingots, French wine bottles and lumps of coal.

National Cycle Network route 55 starts at Coalport and uses a section of the L&NW railway which passes in front of the inn. NCN route 45 (The Mercian Way) is on the other side of the river and uses the old GWR line.

GOLDSTONE: *WHARF TAVERN*

Wharf Tavern, Goldstone, Near Cheswardine, TF9 2LP – 01630 661226
www.wharftaverngoldstone.com

Leave the A41 at Hinstock and take the A529 Wood Lane. Turn off on to local roads at Lockleywood and follow signs for Cheswardine, for just over a mile. Bus route between Market Drayton and Newport. By canal, Shropshire Union (Main Line) between Norbury Junction and Market Drayton, bridge number 55 Goldstone Bridge, moorings and winding hole.

Tucked away in a remote part of north-east Shropshire close to the Staffordshire border is the well-hidden Wharf Tavern, facing the Shropshire Union Canal. It is a popular stopping-off place for visitors on and off the water. Close by, in the same parish of Cheswardine, are two other historic pubs: the Red Lion brew pub at Cheswardine (see chapter 1) a mile away, and the Three Horseshoes, a village local at Sambrook 3 miles away (see chapter 2). Both are easily reached on foot, on quiet lanes, footpaths and along the canal towpath. The Wharf Tavern has two caravan sites – open all year round – (one behind the public house adjacent to the canal and the other opposite the tavern), with electricity, water and waste facilities available. In addition, the pub offers for rent a canal-edge cottage that sleeps four with all mod cons – but no pets allowed. Outside on a summer evening the canalside terrace and garden lawns make for an ideal location to take refreshment and meals, rural and peaceful with just an occasional boat passing by.

The Wharf Tavern's stunning canalside aspect.

In the bar, with central hearth between the bar and restaurant.

The Wharf's sign by the canal – very much a necessity since many of the pub's customers arrive by water.

The Birmingham & Liverpool Junction Canal from Autherley Junction, Wolverhampton, to the Ellesmere & Chester Canal at Nantwich was the last great canal engineered by Thomas Telford, conceived as an important link between the West Midlands and Merseyside. The canal later became part of the Shropshire Union. This portion of the canal was than called the 'main line'. Commercial traffic, able to fend off some of the railway competition, survived on the main line into the 1950s. The main line of the Shropshire Union now passes more boats each year than it did in the height of the freight-carrying era, making the Wharf Tavern a very popular and well-frequented stop. Inside the lounge bar is a long counter which takes up the whole side of the room on the opposite side to the windows. The round tables, cushioned wall seats and carpeted floors give the room an altogether modern feel, although the wood burner and central fireplace at one end of the room are more traditional. The newly refurbished restaurant caters for large groups of people, including holiday boaters and caravan site holidaymakers, with a good selection of cask-conditioned beers, wines and spirits, home-cooked meals in the bar and lounge restaurant with specialities – steak and fresh fish dishes.

HINDFORD: *THE JACK MYTTON INN*

High Street, Hindford, SY11 4NL – 01691 679861
www.jack-mytton.co.uk

Turn off A495 Ellesmere road over a mile north from Whittington, bus route between Oswestry and Ellesmere. By water, take the Llangollen Canal north of bridge 11.

> 'It was his largeness of heart that ruined Mr Mytton, added to the lofty pride which disdained the littleness of Prudence.'
>
> Nimrod, Charles James Apperley,
> *The Memoirs of the Life of the Late John Mytton, Esquire, of Halston*

The Jack Mytton Inn at Hindford is a converted Victorian farmhouse set back from the Llangollen Canal. It is an ideal place for boaters to moor up and for villagers, walkers and holidaymakers to relax and enjoy the countryside. The bar and restaurants offer a choice of real ale and locally sourced seasonal meals. The main bar is separate from the restaurant areas with rustic stone walls and a single bar counter. Next to the bar is a carpeted lounge with sofas and a corner fireplace while an archway leads to the restaurant and dining room, which is laid out with wooden tables and chairs. Adjoining it is a more spacious and airy conservatory dining area, which looks out onto the gardens. When the weather is clement, an outdoor bar is set up to cater for summer visitors or social functions.

The pub takes its name from John (Jack) Mytton (1796–1834) known to all as 'Mad Jack Mytton'. A true prodigal son, Jack's is an extraordinary tale of wanton excess, squandering, wastefulness, spendthrift and drunkenness leading to an early death

The Jack Mytton Inn from the Llangollen Canal.

Light and airy dining area.

Mad Jack kept the bear called Nell as a pet. Jack's biographer, Nimrod, Charles James Apperley, regales us with an anecdote. 'He once rode this bear into his drawing-room, in full hunting costume. The bear carried him very quietly for a time; but on being pricked by the spur, he bit his rider through the calf of his leg.'

– although he is Shropshire's best-remembered sportsman, huntsman and eccentric. Jack lived less than a mile away at Halston Hall, the country seat of the Myttons from 1560. Jack's antics began at an early age. Expelled from Westminster School for fighting the masters, he left Harrow after only three days. His private tutors fared no better, suffering endless practical jokes including finding a horse in one tutor's bedroom. Despite limited academic achievement, Jack managed to get into Cambridge University, immediately started drinking and left without graduating. Like most of the landed gentry of the time, he embarked on the 'The Grand Tour' of Europe and on his return bought a commission in the army, gambling and drinking before resigning. He then claimed his inheritance, which was held in trust until he reached the age of twenty-one years, a fortune from his father who died young at thirty when Jack was just two years of age.

Landlord Ian Spencer Brown chats with local blacksmith Chris Stokes at the bar.

Twice married, his first wife died in 1820, his second wife, Caroline, ran away; both bore him children. In 1819, he bought his way into parliament as MP for Shrewsbury although he only attended the house once, preferring to indulge in horseracing and gambling. From boyhood, Jack hunted foxes with his own pack of hounds, in all kinds of weather. His hunting wardrobe consisted of hundreds of pairs of hunting breeches, hunting boots and thousands of shirts and hats – an excess considering that he normally only wore a light jacket, thin shoes, linen trousers and silk stockings or, sometimes, he even rode naked. Numerous pets roamed the manor including cats, foxhounds, gun dogs, pointers and retrievers. Some even wore costumes. However, Jack was no animal lover. He frequented dogfights and gambled on the outcome. He once fought his own bulldog with his bare fists, bit a mastiff holding it in his own jaws, and was rumoured to have thrown his wife's pet dog on the fire in a rage, burning it alive.

Mad Jack sought thrills driving his four-horse gig furiously around country lanes and once tried to jump over a tollgate with a carriage. He played pranks on visitors to Halston Hall, on one occasion arriving at a dinner party riding his pet bear. Jack drank eight bottles of port a day with brandy and often drank quarts of ale with his tenants. He was a total spendthrift and in fifteen years managed to spend his entire inheritance. In 1830, he fled to France to avoid his creditors, prison and court. One of his final antics was to cure his hiccups by setting light to his shirt and engulfing himself in flames; only the intervention of his friends spared him from serious burns, his comment being 'The hiccup is gone, by God!' Jack returned to England and ended up in Southwark debtors' prison where he died from sheer excess, but ever-popular. More than three thousand people turned out to mourn at his funeral, and the Mytton Inn celebrates and commemorates Jack, their local squire.

MAESBURY MARSH; *NAVIGATION INN*

Maesbury Marsh, Oswestry, SY10 8JB – 01691 672958

Leave the A483 and travel south on the Maesbury Road for just under 2 miles. The pub has a car park.

The Shropshire Union Canal in the north-west of the county was formed by the amalgamation of the Chester and Ellesmere canals in the 1790s. The Ellesmere Canal Company's ambitious plan to link the rivers Mersey, Dee and Severn would have permitted boats to travel between Liverpool and Bristol. A branch ran to Llangollen from Welsh Frankton crossing two impressive aqueducts, the first at Chirk over the River Ceiriog and the other, more famous, at Pontcysyllte over the River Dee. The canal from Frankton to Llanymynech, which opened in 1796, proved a commercial success, especially for the transport of limestone from quarries at Llanymynech, and the Ellesmere canal did succeed in joining the rivers Mersey and Dee. However, its attempt to make a connection with Shrewsbury and the Severn proved unsuccessful, the new cut going no further than Weston Lullingfields. The Ellesmere Canal became part of the Shropshire Union in 1846, which afterwards operated over 200 miles of waterways including the Lower Frankton to Newtown Canal, later referred to as the Montgomeryshire Canal. Competition from the railways inevitably led to a decline in trade for the whole of the Shropshire Union system. Through traffic unexpectedly ceased on the Montgomeryshire Canal when, in 1936, a breach below Frankton cut the canal off from the rest of the system. Repair costs exceeded the annual revenue for the arm prompting legal abandonment in 1944. The line from Llangollen remained open.

The Navigation Inn from the roadside, Maesbury Marsh.

The Navigation
Inn's canalside
aspect.

The magnificent
fireplace.

The Navigation Inn, or the 'Navvy' as it is known locally, is a fine example of a moderately
sized canalside pub, built at the same time as the Montgomeryshire Canal to serve the
busy inland port of Oswestry. By the 1890s, the Navigation Inn had a brewhouse, stabling
and accommodation, and was classed as a roadside inn with five bedrooms. The pub
stands beside the canal wharf and the road to Oswestry, which was once a busy, bustling
interchange between carts and boats. The canal company itself employed a two-horse
dray, two porters and a drayman to transport goods by road to Oswestry. There were daily
deliveries of milk and cheese boated in from Ellesmere. Salt came from Cheshire, ironwork
from Coalbrookdale and coal from Chirk and Ruabon. The life of a boatman in the heyday
of the canal era was tiring and lonely and the 'Navvy' offered a much-needed place to rest,
meet people and socialise. The pub also had overnight stabling facilities for the boatman's
horse. It was not, however, always a genial place for socialising; disputes between local
men and boatmen were frequent and often ended up in fistfights in the adjoining fields
outside the pub.

Joint owner Brent Ellis, presiding in the bar room. . .

. . . in the same bar, a pew from a Carthusian monastery – a perfect substitute settle.

The Navigation, refurbished over the years, has a converted warehouse providing comfortable dining areas for a new generation of boaters, walkers and visitors arriving by car. The pub offers a place to eat, drink and enjoy the canalside view from either the restaurant or terrace. A good range of real ale is available in two bars with separate counters. Seasonal meals prepared with local produce is served in the bars as well as the restaurant, and each bar has comfortable seating and open fires for cold winter days.

Road bridge number 79 crosses the canal between the 'Navvy' and the former wharf. The remains of an old wharf crane, once used at a warehouse destroyed by fire in 1968, are next to the British Waterways sanitary station. This section of the Montgomeryshire Canal is connected to the national network (opened to navigation in spring 2003) and, as restoration continues, the day is nearing when the entire length as far as Welshpool will be navigable. Presently the arm is open to boat traffic from the Llangollen Canal only and the number of boats using it is restricted.

TRENCH: *THE BLUE PIG*

Capewell Road, Trench, Telford, TF2 6QQ – 01952 603527

From the A442 Queensway take the B4373 Trench turn off, next left into Wombridge Road and a housing estate. After ¼ of a mile turn left into Teagues Crescent, left again after a further ¼ mile into Juniper Drive and immediately right into Capewell Road. The pub is at the bottom of the road.

The Blue Pig, formerly the Shropshire Arms, stands next to Trench Pool, a canal reservoir which once supplied water to the Shrewsbury Canal, a branch of the Shropshire Union Canal. Nearby is a large 1960s housing estate and the busy Queensway bypass. In earlier years, the Blue Pig was a true canalside pub, serving customers who worked the canal and inclined plane. The pub remains isolated from other buildings, but it is still a popular local serving the nearby community, and it witnessed the passing of the Industrial Revolution and the canal age.

Trench is a suburb of Telford in the Borough of Telford and Wrekin, north of Oakengates. It was once an area of heavy industry, surrounded by a forest of factory chimneys and smoke-billowing blast furnaces. Above Trench lie Wrockwardine Wood and Donnington Wood, both areas mined extensively for iron ore and coal and where bottle-shaped kilns of a glass works made crown glass bottles for the French wine trade during the latter part of the eighteenth century.

It was difficult to transport the huge amount of minerals and fuel needed to supply these industries before the arrival of railways. The area was very hilly and did not lend itself to the construction of conventional canals able to accommodate the typical wooden narrowboat and butty. Instead, an extensive network of narrower canals evolved and trains of horse-drawn tub-boats, tied together and loaded with raw materials, iron ingots and manufactured goods, moved principally between the mines and iron works in the district. Manufactured goods found their way to the River Severn for transfer to trows at Coalport.

The Blue Pig, Trench. The roadway is where the former canal connected to the inclined plane.

Landlady Susan
Maher serving
early evening
regulars.

The canal
feeder – the only
tangible reminder
of the canal.

The plentiful local supply of coal and manufactured goods also found a ready market at Shrewsbury, transported for a time by packhorse or waggon along the turnpikes. The heavy traffic moved off the roads after Josiah Clowes and later Thomas Telford constructed the Shrewsbury Canal to run from the foot of the Trench Inclined Plane to a basin at Shrewsbury. The inclined plain was 243ft long and lifted tub-boats 70ft, thereby giving the Shrewsbury Canal Company access to the lucrative traffic on the Donnington Wood and Shropshire Canal. An engine house at the head of the inclined plane noisily hauled each heavy tub-boat in a special cradle along rails. This went on for 126 years until it closed in 1921 – the last operational inclined plane in the country.

The corner of the pub which once faced the busy inclined plane. It raised the Shrewsbury Canal to the level of the Wombridge Canal and carried tub-boats on large wooden cradles on a double railway – no trace of it remains.

The inclined plane was long silent by the time the section of canal in front of the Blue Pig finally closed in 1944. Elsewhere, parts remained in water. The stretch in front of the pub disappeared under the Queensway bypass, built in the late 1970s, after which time the pub changed its name to the Blue Pig, adopted from the name of a nearby off-licence. The origins of the name come from the ironmaking traditions of the area. Blue pig is slag, skimmed off molten iron in a blast furnace after it has congealed into a bluish glassy ingot. The pub serves breakfasts during fishing competitions at the reservoir and pints in the public bar. The spacious lounge is well suited to meetings of the Blue Pig Angling Club whose members look after and fish a stretch of the nearby Newport Canal, and in this respect preserve the pub's link with its canal heritage. The Silkin Way passes in front of the pub, following the route of the dry, east Shropshire canal beds and disused railways between Bratton and Coalport.

Railway Pubs

Shropshire's place in railway history is significant. Many of the features of railways as we know them today had their origin in the county. The east Shropshire coalfields and iron works, served by a complex system of tramways, used horses to pull a number of waggons at a time. Coupled together, they formed the first trains. In 1802, Richard Trevithick built the first steam locomotive at the Coalbrookdale works, although it was never completed. Two years later his engine at Penydarren in South Wales became the first to pull a train of waggons on iron rails. Shrewsbury had become the centre of the railways of Shropshire when it joined to the expanding national network of railways in 1848, from the north by the Shrewsbury & Chester Railway while communication to the Midlands came with the Shrewsbury & Birmingham railway sharing lines with the SUR&CC.

The principal railway companies in Shropshire were the London & North Western Railway (L&NWR) and the Great Western Railway (GWR), operating joint lines and sharing the station at Shrewsbury. The other main company in the county, Cambrian Railways, operated services between Whitchurch, Oswestry and North Wales. There were also a number of quirky and unusual railways in Shropshire which still hold a great fascination for railway enthusiasts such as the Cleobury Mortimer & Ditton Priors Light Railway (CM&DP), the Bishop's Castle Railway, Snailbeach District Railways and the much-loved Shropshire & Montgomeryshire Light Railway. The CM&DP joined the GWR at the grouping in 1923; the others stayed independent. The two post-grouping companies in Shropshire were then the GWR (which was the only company not to lose its identity after the mergers) and the London Midland & Scottish railway (LMS) which absorbed the L&NWR. They both became part of British Railways (BR) after nationalisation in 1949. Like the canals before them, the railways also declined, hastened by road competition and lack of investment. Many branch lines and stations closed in the 1960s under the Beeching Report, leaving a much-depleted railway system in the county and many railway pubs without a passing clientele. The railway pubs included in this chapter are survivors of the railway age. Some still serve the railway traveller as they once did in the heyday of the railways. Where the railway has long gone, others prove that a railway once existed by including 'Railway', 'Station' or 'Railwayman' in their name.

A view from the locomotive footplate as the engine pauses outside the Railwaymans Arms at Bridgnorth SVR station.

BRIDGNORTH: *RAILWAYMANS ARMS*

Platform 1, SVR Station, Hollybush Road, Bridgnorth, WV16 5DT – 01746 764361
www.bridgnorthstation.co.uk

Follow Road signs for Severn Valley Railway, turn off Hollybush Road B4363 into Station Lane. Alternatively abandon the car – arrive by train on the preserved Severn Valley Railway – the railway runs trains that connect at various times with the national rail network service at Kidderminster. Bus stop adjacent to SVR car park (mostly drop-off), routes to principal towns in Shropshire, Kidderminster, Wolverhampton and the Black Country from High Town & Low Town.

The Railwaymans Arms has the enviable accolade of the station refreshment room that never closes – even when the railway services were withdrawn by BR in the early 1960s. Bridgnorth was once a through-station on a rail route which connected Shrewsbury with the Oxford, Worcester & Wolverhampton line at Hartlebury and Kidderminster. The GWR, and later BR, owned both lines. The decline in railway traffic and receipts on this route inevitably brought about closure and withdrawal of services. However, the far-sighted ambitions of railway enthusiasts and preservationists lead to the successive reopening of the line between Bridgnorth, Bewdley and Kidderminster and the adoption of the line's former name, the Severn Valley Railway (SVR).

The entrance from the station drive to the Railwaymans Arms, Bridgnorth.

The entrance from platform 1.

In the lounge bar.

Today the railway sees thousands of visitors each year and carries more passengers than at any other time in its past. The line operates all year round and services change seasonally. However, in 2007 the railway suffered a tragedy when exceptionally wet conditions and torrential rainstorms brought about extensive washouts of the track formation and cessation of through-services. Only the section between Bewdley and Kidderminster was offering any kind of service; the line through Shropshire was silent. A campaign to raise funds, refurbish and rebuild the line proved successful and the line reopened in record time.

During the enforced closure of the line and loss of services to Kidderminster, pints continued to be pulled in the Railwaymans Arms and the pub lived up to its accolade of the refreshment room that never closes. The pub is open even if the railway is not running. It attracts visitors to the railway but also has its regular clientele comprising of off-duty railway personnel, volunteers, locals and real ale enthusiasts; a pleasant and friendly mix of people young and old alike. The pub sells Bathams beer, guest beers, lagers, cider and excellent pork pies. Around the walls there is a wealth of railway paraphernalia, which includes station totems, locomotive smokebox and cabside number plates, railway paintings and photographs.

The Railwaymans Arms,
Bridgnorth.

IRONBRIDGE: *STATION HOTEL*

Ladywood Road, Ironbridge, Telford, TF8 7JU – 01952 882407

Use pay and display car park south of the Iron Bridge. Bus routes between Shrewsbury, Bridgnorth and Telford from town centre.

The Station Hotel is a large, blue, brick-built building next to the site on which Ironbridge and Broseley station once stood. It was originally a railway hostelry for the former Severn Valley Railway on the southern side of the River Severn, in sight of the Iron Bridge. The SVR was conceived as a branch line from Worcester (and Hartlebury Junction) to Shrewsbury and the 40-mile route followed the River Severn for most of the way. Ironbridge and Broseley station opened to passengers with the whole line in 1862. The railway was taken over by the GWR in 1872 and BR closed it in 1963. The station buildings languished around for some years before being demolished. The site was cleared and turned into a car park. This northern section of the line – lifted entirely above Bridgnorth – was less fortunate than the sections between Kidderminster and Bridgnorth where the track was preserved and reinstated as a steam railway by the efforts of the Severn Valley Railway Society, formed in 1965. Little evidence of a railway ever being at Ironbridge exists apart from a retaining wall, some rusty rails embedded in the road leading up from the Iron Bridge and a solitary level-crossing gatepost. Apart from a railway bridge nearby, the only tangible sign of the former railway is the Station Hotel.

The Station Hotel, Ironbridge – a former railway pub.

Inside the single bar.

Almost a contemporary of the railway, the hotel is built of the same engineering bricks used to retain the road alongside the station and the railway embankment above the river. The main part of the building stands three storeys high with two main doors leading to an open-plan single bar. The interior is much altered having received a typical 1970s and 1980s makeover, which does little to enhance the remaining historical features of the pub. The bar counter is modern as are the tables and chairs, although there is a welcoming real fireplace at one end of the room. However, outside, the substantial fabric of the building – its roof, heavy doors, the stone sills and lintels in the window openings – strongly suggests a railway building. This is especially true when viewed from the pub's comfortable umbrella-covered seating areas under the pub sign depicting Stephenson's *Rocket* and in view of Abraham Darby's Iron Bridge. In stark contrast to the preserved heritage SVR line south of Bridgnorth, the railway preservation movement has shown little interest in reinstating railway features, buildings or track on the site of the former Ironbridge station, although the benefits for the thousands of visitors to this World Heritage Site of a preserved railway attraction or operating a novel park-and-ride service on a reinstated section of railway are obvious. In the meantime, the track bed remains and passes in front of the pub, part of the Mercian Way National Cycle Route 45, which runs from Chester to Salisbury. The Station Hotel is a welcome pit stop for a break from cycling, a place to enjoy a pint and have a meal during the day or early evening. Similarly, the Severn Way footpath crosses at the Iron Bridge and passes in front of the pub, offering the long-distance walker the same opportunity. In the evenings, the pub changes its role to a busy local with live entertainment and quiz nights.

OAKENGATES: *STATION HOTEL*

42 Market Street, Oakengates, Telford, TF2 6DU – 01952 612949

Use town centre car parks, a short walk to the railway station.

O akengates derives its name from a combination of early British and Norse words broadly meaning 'the road at the meeting of the valley'. The town during the Middle Ages was little more than a hamlet with a holy well dedicated to Mammon (greed and avarice). The well may have contained alum, a mordant used in dyeing cloth which was much needed in Shrewsbury for its wool trade.

The late eighteenth century saw the arrival of heavy industries into the district and the mining of coal, ironstone and limestone, initially transported to local ironworks on the east Shropshire canals. The first railway arrived at Oakengates in 1849: the Shrewsbury & Birmingham Railway, a broad gauge line delayed by three years because of difficulties building the 471-yard stretch of tunnel on the outskirts of the town. The line became part of the GWR in 1854. The railway tunnel passed under the summit level of the Shropshire Canal. Disaster struck in 1855 when a breach drained the entire canal into the tunnel, causing flooding in the town.

Another Station Hotel, Oakengates, still serving rail travellers.

In the bar.

The back bar – a repository of local history and no better place to study Oakengates' past.

Another railway, the Coalport branch of the L&NWR, came through the town in 1861, replacing the greater part of the partially disused Shropshire Canal. The railway closed in 1964. Increasing trade and commerce brought by the railways gave rise to growth in the town and its population and businesses, shops, and hotels prospered. The railways also gave impetus to an increase in the number of pubs in the town centre and by the 1890s there were no fewer than ten. Three establishments in Market Street catered for railway customers: the Train Inn, which closed in the 1960s, the Station Inn that closed much earlier in 1934 and an earlier namesake the Station Hotel that closed in 1860 before the arrival of the L&NWR Coalport line.

It was commonplace for ordinary householders to convert their homes to a 'public alehouse' to provide a second income with the licensee retaining his previous job. Henry Harrison, manager of the Hollinswood Iron Works, converted his home in this way during 1868, calling it the Station Hotel. Ann Harrison held the licence until 1880. The pub closed for five years from 1896 after Isaac Harris was landlord. In 1901, William Butler and Co., of Wolverhampton, bought the pub and the tenant landlord was Samuel Shinger. Butlers merged into Mitchell's & Butlers, Birmingham, in 1960 and later the company merged with Bass in 1961. The Station Hotel was then sold to landlord George Muntar in 1988.

In recent times, the pub has appeared in the CAMRA *Good Beer Guide* and holds regular beer festivals throughout the year. The lounge bar has been converted into the Oakengates room with literally wall-to-wall history of the town, which makes for fascinating reading over a pint. The public bar has a large real fireplace and comfortable seating. The wooden bar counter has eight hand-pulls, each with a different bitter or mild, along with additional pumps for stout, lager, cider and perry. The bar has a GWR theme with a painted sign at the bar and numerous items of railway interest.

The well-stocked bar with a variety of different beers to choose from.

YORTON: *THE RAILWAY INN*

Wayside, Yorton, SY4 3EP – 01939 220240

Next to Yorton station on the Shrewsbury to Crewe line, 1 mile from the B5476 Wem Road.

T he pub stands next to Yorton railway station (opened in 1858 by the L&NWR) on the Shrewsbury–Crewe line. It is a free house owned and run by licensee Liz Newnes who is continuing the family business started in the mid-1930s. Liz's grandfather, a former gamekeeper at Sandford Hall near Prees, together with his wife and four daughters took over the tenancy in 1937 when Southam's Brewery of Shrewsbury, later Whitbread, owned the pub. The tenancy was transferred from Grandfather Robinson – an imposing 6ft and 22 stone man – to his eldest daughter and then to granddaughter Liz in 1971, now the surviving member of the family after the death of her mother Alice in October 2008. Alice lived and worked at the pub for seventy-one years and kept the smallholding next to the pub, supplying milk to local dairies. Milking cows each morning before setting off to school while her elder sister ran the pub, Alice continued to work the smallholding after she got married.

Yorton Railway Inn, from the station entrance . . .

. . . and looking on from the embankment. The pub has 'Hotel' written on the gable facing the railway line, placed there over seventy years ago in an attempt to drum up trade from the railway. Beer was given away free for a month as a promotion – although the pub was never a hotel.

The lounge is also the
domain of 'Pinkie' who
resides in a glass case
on the wall – a fish
weighing 40lbs 4oz
caught by the Grinshill
& Fenemer Angling Club
on 28 August 1992.

The bar with well-stoked fire.

The couple lived at the pub and Liz Newnes was born in an upstairs room. Landlady Liz
and villagers recall how each cow had its own name and how bales of hay delivered to
the smallholding were paid for with a pint of beer.

At one time it was normal practise to hand down licenced premises through the
family, from one generation to the next, something which is very rare today when pub
tenancy is measured by months and the majority of pubs are rented or managed. It is
even rarer to see a pub change little over three generations. The Railway Inn is such a
pub. Its décor belongs to an unhurried and relaxed age, unchanged from the mid-1930s.
The public bar has its original wooden serving counter and traditional hand-pulls and
there is a red quarry-tiled floor and open fireplace, over which hangs a round clock
which bears scorch marks around its wooden casing, testimony to an incident years ago
when Alice over-zealously poured paraffin into the fireplace to kindle the fire. The bar
has a dartboard with a shelf of shields and trophies, and pictures and mirrors on plain
walls, and dominoes is still played in a corner.

The adjoining carpeted lounge has a 1950s feel with a well-stoked coal fire at one end
and comfortable padded chairs. It is a perfect retreat for the numerous clubs, societies
and charities that use the room for meetings.

Another glance at this unspoilt pub.

Liz tells of how during the Second World War there was a narrow escape for a train travelling from Shrewsbury, stalked by a German aircraft. The engine driver, aware of the threat, stopped his train in a wooded area for cover. The aircraft was unable to pursue the attack and was later shot down by locally based fighters. The pub was a haven for soldiers camped out nearby who sometimes came in from the cold to write letters home. Landlord Robinson was sympathetic, having served in the First World War, and understood the hardships of living under canvas. However, servicemen did not necessarily get on with each other, especially local infantrymen and RAF servicemen from nearby Shropshire airbases. Allegedly, during a battle the RAF failed to give air support to the infantry, which sparked off a dispute. Afterwards, bad feelings continued, resulting in Army men and RAF men segregating to the bar or lounge to avoid speaking to each other.

In 1973 an incident occurred on the bridge overlooking the pub. A diesel locomotive caught fire at the station and the driver brought it to rest over the bridge, the fire brigade came to put out the flames. Former railway workers and train drivers still regularly meet at the pub and the station is still open as a request stop – by a hand signal to the driver to board or by informing the conductor to alight. The Marches Way long-distance footpath from Chester crosses the lane in front of the pub and part of the Shropshire Way passes near Grinshill Hill and the picturesque village of Clive. The Railway Inn is an ideal place to end a day's walking and exploration and is also the ideal place to stop off for a while on a railway journey.

ACKNOWLEDGEMENTS

I would like to thank all the publicans, owners, managers, tenants and staff of the pubs that I visited for their willing and enthusiastic help in answering my questions, and for agreeing to me taking photographs. I was able to include many interesting anecdotes and snippets of information, which I would never have been able to find in published records. I am especially grateful to customers who were most willing to discuss their pubs. Loyal and supportive of their landlord, all were appreciative of the unique historic character of their local and the service it performs in their community. I would also like to thank the owners and employees of Shropshire's breweries – fourteen at the last count. They are a credit to their profession, keen and committed to the real ale product.

In addition, my thanks to my fellow researchers Mark and Lynn Holmes, a licensee said, 'Lynn is the landlord's perfect customer, she drives men to drink and then drives them back again.' My thanks also to John and Maria Hawkins, Barry Bull, Frank Bonny and Roy Andrews, who accompanied me on a number of excursions and shared their opinions along with the odd pint or two, or three! In addition, special thanks to the members of CAMRA that I inevitably met on my travels; their comments were invaluable. Finally an extra special thanks to my wife Karen for her encouragement and forbearance. Published sources consulted include county and local histories, town and country guides, CAMRA *Good Beer Guide* (back issues from 1975 to 2008), trade directories, historical maps and sundry histories of pubs and inns.

Looking on while his master takes leave for a cigarette.